ADVANCE PRAISE FOR

The Emotional Inte

"Emotional intelligence is an extremely important skill to have for personal and professional success. This book is excellent. . . . I strongly recommend it."

—Ken Blanchard, bestselling business book author of all time; coauthor of *The One Minute Manager*

"This book is filled with wisdom, inspiration, and practical advice, rooted in groundbreaking research. The authors' positive strategies are immensely powerful and will change the way you look at your life, your work, and the world."

—Captain D. Michael Abrashoff, author of the bestseller *It's Your Ship* and *Get Your Ship Together*

"In the fast lane of business life today, people spend more time on computer keyboards, BlackBerries, and conference calls than they do in face-to-face communication. We're expected to piece together broken conversations, cryptic voice mails, and abbreviated text messages to figure out how to proceed. In this increasingly complex web, emotional intelligence is more important than ever before. This book is filled with invaluable insights and information that no one can afford to ignore."

—Rajeev Peshawaria, executive director, Goldman Sachs International

"I distributed the *Quick Book* to my team. We found it very helpful in our dealings with each other and our internal customers. . . . If your desire is to be a leader people will trust and follow, this book provides an opportunity that can not only change your professional career but also your personal relationships."

—Regina Sacha, vice president, human resources, FedEx Custom Critical

"Drs. Bradberry and Greaves have created a gem that is powerful and easy to read. This book provides a captivating look at the things that matter most in life. Succeeding in Hollywood is as tough as any business, and emotional intelligence skills are essential. I highly recommend this book."

—Matt Olmstead, executive producer, ABC's *NYPD Blue* and *Blind Justice*

"At last a book that gives how to's rather than just what to's. We need no more convincing that emotional intelligence is at the core of life success. What we need are practical ways of improving it. Bradberry and Greaves' brilliant new book is a godsend. It will change your life."

—Joseph Grenny, *New York Times* bestselling coauthor of *Crucial Conversations* and *Crucial Confrontations*

"This book is a wake-up call for anyone who wants to dramatically improve their work life and strengthen their relationships. Drs. Bradberry and Greaves offer powerful research, practical strategies, and fascinating stories that will transform the way we think about ourselves and how we interact with those we care about the most."

—Jim Loehr, *New York Times* bestselling author, *The Power of Full Engagement* and *Stress for Success*

"This is a wonderful, practical, helpful book full of tools and techniques you can use to get along better with all the people in your life."

—Brian Tracy, bestselling author,
Eat That Frog and *TurboCoach*

"Emotional intelligence is such a crucial concept to understand—yet so many people are unaware of it. The authors do a magnificent job of explaining the incredible power of emotional intelligence and how to apply it to achieve your ultimate goals. I've used this book to maximize my potential and I recommend it to anyone who desires to be truly successful."

—Richard La China, CEO of iTECH,
1999 Ernst & Young Entrepreneur of the Year

"Whip out your pen and get ready to take copious notes. This wonderful gem of a book is chock-a-block full of invaluable insights and incredibly useful suggestions—backed by strong scientific evidence. Word for word this is the most precious book I've read in a long time. I will give it to all my friends and clients as the one 'must read' for the season."

—Jim Belasco, *New York Times* bestselling coauthor,
Flight of the Buffalo

"My clients tend to be very successful and incredibly busy. This book delivers valuable insights without wasting time! My coaches and I have done powerful work aided by this book and the emotional intelligence test that comes with it. A fantastic combination for learning the skills that are critical to high job performance."

—Marshall Goldsmith, bestselling author and premier executive educator, as ranked by *Forbes, The Wall Street Journal, The Harvard Business Review,* and *Fast Company*

"Drs. Bradberry and Greaves have succeeded in creating a practical summary of emotional intelligence. Without being simplistic, the *Quick Book* is accessible to managers and employees who need a quick yet sophisticated understanding of the topic. This book and TalentSmart® e-learning are important components of Nokia's management and employee development programs."

—Jennifer Tsoulos, M.S., human resources,
Nokia Mobile Phones

"This book is a great resource for those of us charged with providing emergency services to the public. Through the simple and effective steps outlined in the *Quick Book,* I was able to learn and subsequently put into practice the emotional intelligence skills necessary to better relate to my customers during crisis situations. The section on emotionally intelligent teams is a tool most supervisors should find useful in facilitating teamwork and promoting esprit de corps."

—Dominick Arena, fire captain,
City of Escondido, California, Fire Department

A Fireside Book
Published by Simon & Schuster
New York London Toronto Sydney

The Emotional Intelligence Quick Book

EVERYTHING YOU
NEED TO KNOW
TO PUT YOUR **EQ** TO WORK

Travis Bradberry
and Jean Greaves

FIRESIDE
Rockefeller Center
1230 Avenue of the Americas
New York, NY 10020

This Fireside Edition 2005

Designed by William Ruoto

Manufactured in the United States of America

10 9 8 7 6 5 4 3 2 1

Library of Congress Cataloging-in-Publication Data
Bradberry, Travis.
The emotional intelligence quick book : everything you need to know to put your EQ to work / Travis Bradberry and Jean Greaves.—1st Fireside ed.
p. cm.
Includes bibliographical references and index.
1. Emotional intelligence. I. Greaves, Jean. II. Title.
BF576.B73 2005 152.4—dc22 2005042593

ISBN-13: 978-0-7432-7326-8
ISBN-10: 0-7432-7326-5
ISBN-13: 978-1-4165-4167-7 (Pbk)
ISBN-10: 1-4165-4167-5 (Pbk)

We dedicate this book to E. L. Thorndike, who had the foresight nearly a century ago to tell the world that there is more than IQ

Contents

A *Quick* Note from the Authors

When you profile more than half a million people, distinct trends emerge in the data. It is perfectly reasonable to assume that as you collect more responses, the book should get longer. We found the opposite: as you collect more data, things come together and simplify. It is the same phenomenon our statistics professors preached to us about during graduate school. The findings we have stumbled upon are so pervasive that we have no option but to deliver a book that reflects the succinct, powerful message that has emerged from such a large study of emotional intelligence.

It feels strange to admit that people initially twisted our arms into writing this book, but that is exactly what happened. In dedicating ourselves to the field of emotional intelligence, we never endeavored to write more than the assessment we had initially created. Quite frankly, the book (well . . . books) on emotional intelligence had already been written. We often hold emotional intelligence workshops and speak on the topic. Our emphasis has always been to take this complicated phenomenon and make it attainable and easy to use, even for those who aren't typically interested in "self-help." This has been and continues to be a very fulfilling role for us. The more audiences we have addressed, the more they have asked (sometimes demanded) that we bring our ideas and unique research to life through a book.

You are holding in your hands the result of the now-welcome pressure to make emotional intelligence accessible in a book. It was a remarkable experience translating the results from more than 500,000 people into proven strategies anyone can use. Even though this book is "quick," we take our work very seriously. Emotional intelligence is a highly important skill that countless individuals have embraced to their benefit. Therefore, every story you read in this book does more than prove a point. They are all real, thoroughly detailed, and carefully researched. Emotional intelligence is such a powerful part of everyday life that we don't have to look far to find a good story and we certainly don't need to make them up.

We are also pleased to offer you additional insight into your emotional intelligence through the Emotional Intelligence Appraisal. This test can serve as your foundation to discover where you stand today and where you should head in applying the emotional intelligence skills you learn in the book. Emotional intelligence is a dynamic, yet practical, concept. With the right understanding and focus, new skills can be learned relatively quickly with impressive results. If you practice and polish your skills over time, you will ensure a lasting change from your efforts.

The Emotional Intelligence Quick Book takes a bold new step by providing a speedy overview of emotional intelligence in an applied, how-to format. Enjoy the journey. This first stride will be a quick one, but the impact from what you learn may change your life.

Warmly,
Travis and Jean
San Diego, California

P.S. We look forward to hearing from *Quick Book* readers. Your letters and e-mails are our only way to know if the book helps. Feel free to contact us at the addresses listed below.

To contact the authors via e-mail:
Dr. Travis Bradberry: tbradberry@talentsmart.com
Dr. Jean Greaves: jgreaves@talentsmart.com

To contact the authors via regular mail:

TalentSmart Quick Book Feedback—Suite G
11526 Sorrento Valley Road
San Diego, CA 92121

Foreword

Not education. Not experience. Not knowledge or intellectual horsepower. None of these serve as an adequate predictor of why one person succeeds and another doesn't. There is something else going on that society doesn't seem to account for.

We see examples of this every day in our workplaces, homes, churches, schools, and neighborhoods. We observe supposedly brilliant and well-educated people struggle while others with fewer obvious skills or attributes flourish. And we ask ourselves why?

The answer almost always has to do with this concept called emotional intelligence. And while it is harder to identify and measure than IQ or experience, and certainly more difficult to capture on a resume, its power cannot be denied.

And by now, it's not exactly a secret. People have been talking about emotional intelligence for a while, but somehow they haven't been able to harness its power. After all, as a society we continue to focus most of our self-improvement energy in the pursuit of knowledge, experience, intelligence, and education—which would be fine if we could honestly say we had a full understanding of our emotions, not to mention the emotions of others, and how they influence our lives so fundamentally every day.

I think the reason for this gap between the popularity of emotional intelligence as a concept and its application in society is twofold. First, people just don't understand it. They often mistake emotional intelligence for a form of charisma or gregariousness. Second, they don't see it as something that can be improved. Either you have it or you don't.

And that's why this is such a helpful book. By understanding what emotional intelligence really is and how we can manage it in our lives we can begin to leverage all of that intelligence, education, and experience we've been storing up all these years.

So, whether you've been wondering about emotional intelligence for years or know nothing about it, this book can drastically change the way you think about success. You might want to read it twice.

Patrick Lencioni
author of *The Five Dysfunctions of a Team*;
president of the Table Group

ONE

What Is Emotional Intelligence, Really?

Chapter 1

THE DISCOVERY

PHINEAS GAGE

A TRAGIC ACCIDENT UNCOVERS THE SECRETS OF EMOTIONAL INTELLIGENCE (EQ)

◆

Should you think these remarks of sufficient importance to deserve a place in your Journal, they are at your service.

DR. JOHN HARLOW,
to the Boston Medical and Surgical Journal, *1848*

It was frigid and damp at dawn the last day Phineas Gage arrived to work on time. As he shoved his hands in the pockets of his jacket and cut through the cold, he contemplated the challenges that lay ahead in the building of the Burlington Railroad through Vermont. In the eighteen months he'd served as foreman, the crew had made considerable progress, but the terrain they were now forced to conquer was rocky and unforgiving. The early dawn light, softened by the moisture in the air, scarcely lit the winding path to the job site. The distant rhythm of iron sledgehammers thumping in sequence was soothing and forced an early morning smile from Phineas's lips. His crew was on the job a full fifteen minutes before the first whistle. Phineas had earned a reputation as the most efficient and capable foreman in the company. The discipline and passion he brought to the site ensured that projects were completed on time, and the social niceties he espoused made him a favorite with the men he supervised. A "shrewd, smart businessman," he walked his talk, avoided the alluring depravity of the local saloon, and got along famously with family and friends.[1]

The day wore on with the usual efficiency. Yard by yard Phineas and his crew laid tracks, blasting through the rugged terrain in the quest to speed travel for busy commuters. By the time he glanced at his watch at 4:30, they had added half a mile to the rail line. With skill Phineas thrust his tamping iron into the angled blasting hole and entertained thoughts of the day he had retrieved this special rod from the local blacksmith. The brawny craftsman had explained to Phineas with uncharacteristic glee that this iron was unlike any other he had ever seen.

Before taking the next swing in his daily exercise of geometry and strength, Phineas signaled his assistant to pour sand into the blasting hole. The layer of sand would protect the powder from exploding prematurely while he packed it with the tamping iron. As Phineas reared back to swing, he was startled by a shrill racket behind him. Peering over his right shoulder, he saw that the crew in the pit had knocked over a large load of boulders they were transferring to a platform car with a crane. Phineas sighed briefly to mourn the setback, then completed his swing with the iron, oblivious to the fact that his assistant had also been distracted by the noise. The assistant had failed to place sand in the hole, and the scrape of Phineas's iron against the rock perimeter of the crevice created a spark big enough to ignite the unprotected powder at the bottom. The raw force of the explosion launched Phineas's tamping iron like a rocket. It pierced his face below his left eye and continued upward through the top of his head and beyond. The iron finally settled in the weeds a hundred feet from the spot where Phineas stood.

Phineas's body flew backward from the impact and he lay silently for a moment, writhing in shock. A thin whisper of air disguised his overwhelming desire to scream—it was all the noise he could force from his lungs. He could feel the wound below his eye where the thirteen-pound tamping iron—forty-three inches long and a full inch and a quarter in diameter—had thrust itself through his face. He had no sensation of the massive hole the iron had left as it had emerged through the top of his head. The world as he knew it changed forever that afternoon. Phineas's loyal crew rushed to his side and looked into his eyes for any sign of life. They laughed anxiously as Phineas peered up at them and groaned, "I think I'm going to need to see Dr. Harlow." His sense of humor still intact, Phineas let his men load him into an oxcart to take him to town. Sitting upright in the cart on his own, Phineas noticed his assistant walking somberly beside him. He leaned over and made a request typical of any foreman leaving the job site: "Hand me the book, please." Like young boys watching their father perform a Herculean feat of strength, the bemused railroad workers stood in awe as Phineas logged his exit from the job site.

At 5:30 P.M. on Wednesday, September 13, 1848—just one hour after his horrific accident—Phineas Gage stood unassisted on the patio of his home. The local physician, expecting nothing coher-

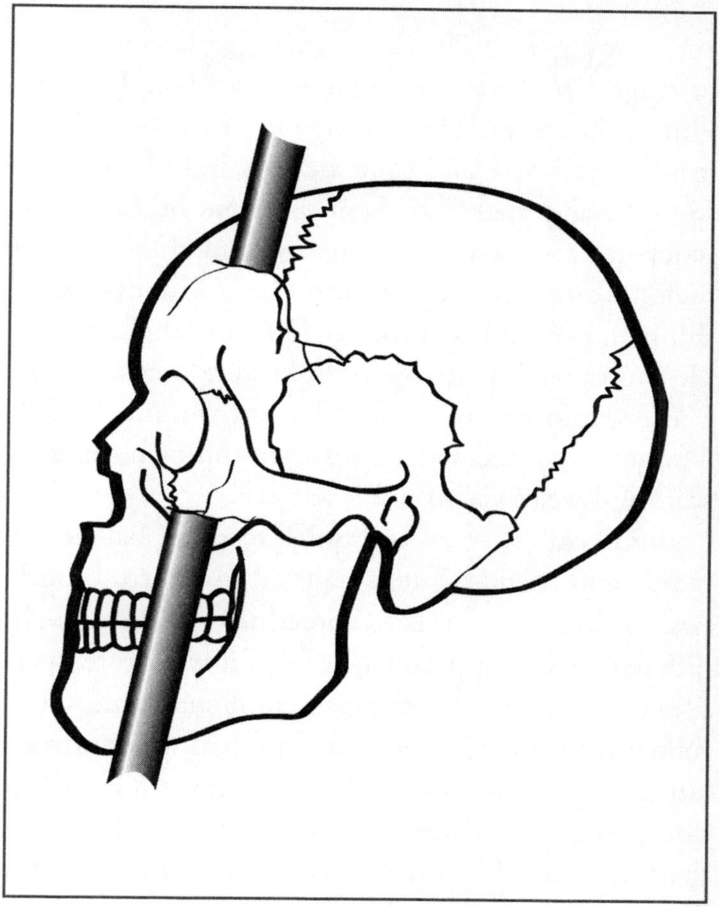

Trajectory of the forty-three-inch tamping iron that traveled through the head of railroad foreman Phineas Gage on September 13, 1848. The iron removed the entire front portion of his brain. His skull and the original iron that went through it are still on public display in the Warren Anatomical Museum at the Harvard Medical School in Boston, Massachusetts.

ent to come from Phineas's lips, asked his crew for a briefing. "Well, here's enough work for you, Doctor," Phineas interrupted before anyone could speak. "The iron entered here and came out my head here." Despite having had the front portion of his brain scooped from his skull much as you might a hunk of melon from the rind at breakfast, Phineas could think and speak just as he could before the accident. He was treated intensely in the coming weeks by Dr. Harlow, and eventually his physical wounds healed. The accident seemed to leave nothing more than scars and weak vision in his left eye.

Phineas's survival and quick recovery baffled his family and friends. But as he tried to return to business as usual, they realized something was hauntingly different. His first peculiar new habit was his temper. He cursed like a sailor and gave conflicting orders that followed his mood. The man who had never arrived late for work was now apathetic about getting the job done. The contractors who had once touted him as their most capable foreman were forced to terminate his employment.

During the eleven years Phineas lived after the accident, he was a transformed man. Dr. Harlow's detailed notes describe a pervasive change in his behavior that could only be explained, literally, by the missing pieces of his mind.

> The effect of the injury appears to have been the destruction of the equilibrium between his intellectual faculties and the animal propensities. He was now capricious, fitful, irreverent, impatient of restraint, vacillating. . . . His physical recovery was complete, but those who knew him as a shrewd, smart, energetic, persistent business man, recognized the change in mental character. The balance of his mind was gone.[2]

To put it bluntly, Phineas's emotional intelligence left his head for good the morning of the accident. In removing the front portion of his brain, the tamping iron took with it his ability to turn his impulses and emotions into reasoned action. Phineas was left a walking, talking, sentient being, yet one with very little self-control. Somehow his intellect remained intact. He could do complicated math problems and understood the logistics of building the railroad. He lived independently, just as he had before the blast. Those he met assumed his rash behavior was just a part of his personality, but previous acquaintances knew differently. They found the new Phineas irrational and erratic. Every urge and feeling seemed to generate impulsive action, and more often than not, it had a disastrous effect on the quality of his life.

The Path Between Feeling and Reason

Phineas's grisly accident continues to baffle us today. His survival was truly a miracle, and the changes in his behavior teach us more about the brain than the most sophisticated technology available can. Modern devices can map the brain to show which areas are most important for different types of thought, but no mechanical gadget can show how a human will behave without the assistance of the front of his brain. Phineas's mishap is more than a fascinating story to tell around the campfire; it shows us something important about how humans think. The daily challenge of dealing effectively with emotions is a critical part of the human condition. Even people with their brains wholly intact can fall victim to irrational behavior.

Unlike Phineas, we have a choice in how we respond to emotions. Each of us takes in information from the world around us through the five senses. Everything we see, smell, hear, taste, and touch travels through the body in the form of electric signals. These signals pass from cell to cell until they reach their ultimate destination, the brain. If a mosquito bites you on the leg, that sensation creates signals that must travel to your brain before you are aware of the pest. Our sensations enter the brain in one place at the back near the spinal cord. Complex, rational thinking happens on the opposite side of the brain, at the front, which is the same part that Phineas lost. When the electric signals enter your brain, they must travel all the way across it before you can have your first logical thought about the event. This chasm in the mind between the entry of our senses and reason is a problem because between the two rests the limbic system. This is the area in the brain where emotions are experienced. Signals passing through the limbic system create an emotional reaction to events before they reach the front of the brain. The front of the brain can't stop the emotion "felt" in the limbic system. Instead, the two areas communicate constantly. This process of communication is the physical source of emotional intelligence.

After his accident, poor Phineas was all emotion. In losing the entire front portion of his brain, he lost his ability to reason about and react to his feelings. Indeed, everything he encountered, every experience he had resulted in a rash emotional response. Phineas had zero ability to manage his feelings or even understand their presence. Every hour of every day Phineas was overcome by his emotions, much the same way you might be if you were being chased by a tiger or trying to help a drowning child. Our brains are wired to make us emotional creatures. The fact that we experience the emotional response to an event first means that our primary feelings are

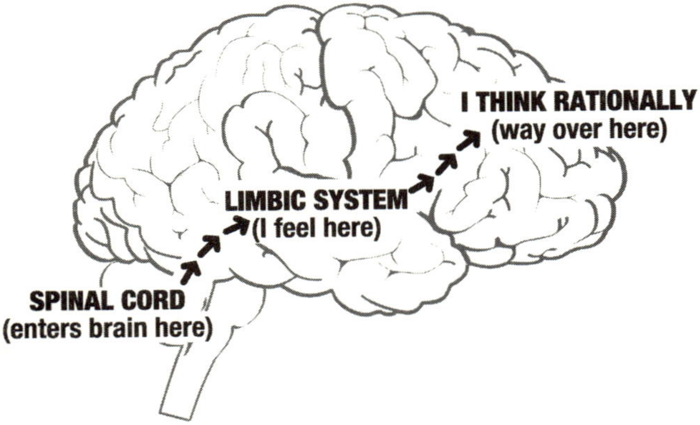

The physical pathway for emotional intelligence starts in the brain, at the spinal cord. Your primary senses enter here and must travel to the front of your brain before you can think rationally about your experience. But first they travel through the limbic system, the place where emotions are experienced. Emotional intelligence requires effective communication between the rational and emotional centers of the brain.

strong motivators of behavior. Some experiences result in emotions that we are easily aware of; other times emotions may seem nonexistent. The location of the limbic system ensures that feelings play a role in every facet of our behavior.

Billions of microscopic neurons line the road between the rational and emotional centers of the brain. Information travels between them much as cars do on a city street. When you practice emotional intelligence, the traffic flows smoothly in both directions. Increases in the traffic strengthen the connection between the rational and emotional centers of the brain. Your emotional intelligence is greatly affected by your ability to keep this road well traveled. The more you think about what you are feeling—and do something productive with that feeling—the more developed this pathway becomes. Some of us struggle along a two-lane country road, while others have built a five-lane superhighway. A generous flow of traffic is the cornerstone of a high emotional intelligence. When too little traffic flows in either direction, the behavior that results is ineffective.

Why do people spend so much time ignoring their feelings or getting run over by them? Most lapses in emotional intelligence come from a simple lack of understanding. You can discover specific skills that empower the use of "smart" behavior in the face of challenges. Harnessing the power of emotional intelligence at work and home is no longer a choice. In order to be successful and fulfilled today, you must learn to maximize these skills, for it is those who employ a unique blend of reason and feeling who achieve the greatest results.

The Other Side of Smart

WHAT DOES EMOTIONAL INTELLIGENCE LOOK LIKE?

◆

Discovery consists of seeing what everybody has seen and thinking what nobody has thought.

—Albert von Szent-Gyorgyi

Lily awoke one sunny Monday morning in San Francisco. She took a shower, got dressed for work, and drank coffee as she read the paper. At times her mind wandered off to thoughts of the rewards of Biotech Bay, the term used to describe the burgeoning biotechnology industry in her area. For many years,

Lily had worked for the same company. She had had no complaints in the beginning, but as time had worn on, her job had grown stagnant. Her enthusiasm for creating drugs to fight cancer remained an important part of her life, but there was little else to motivate her. She performed the same tasks week in and week out, with hardly any opportunity to stretch her skills.

The longer she stayed in that job, the more she realized there was too little communication from management on the issues that mattered most to the people working there. The team in the lab lamented the absence of any real opportunity for career development inside the company. They were stuck in their places like rats. She longed for the chance to grow and do new things. She wanted to be challenged by her work once again. For months, her job had provided nothing but frustration.

But this day was another story: Lily was starting a new position at a different company. She had made the decision to change jobs six weeks prior, when David, her old boss, had invited her to join him in a small start-up. He had left her previous employer, frustrated by the direction the company was headed in. He had convinced her that the new venture would bring her ideas to life in bold new ways.

As Lily flipped open the newspaper to the business section, she suddenly lost her train of thought.

A huge graph of her previous employer's plummeting stock price glared at her from the page. She glanced at her watch, grabbed her coffee, and scuttled out the door.

Lily's first year at the new company was like a day spent in the big city. It was exciting, there were more things to do than she had time for, and she came home exhausted. Just as David had promised, the company grew underneath her rather than above her. She ran the lab that produced new cancer drugs and was often invited to join in discussions about the company's plans for clinical trials. Lily felt privileged to offer her input into the trials, because they would test the effectiveness of new drugs used to treat cancer. David delivered a job with opportunities that were not afforded by Lily's previous employer.

By the middle of her second year in the new job, though, things started to fizzle. Her team in the lab got along well and projects moved quickly, but she was bored. She continued to have opportunities to make recommendations to the executive team on how new drugs should be tested through clinical trials. Occasionally her suggestions were followed, and this made her happy. But the meetings were beginning to look frighteningly similar. She was allowed only a certain level of input into how things should be run. Even as her knowledge became more sophisticated, her best suggestions were ignored. Lily felt frustrated. The executives were doing the important work, planning the drug trials, while she was left to babysit a lab that was essentially running itself. She continued to study the clinical trials, and innovative ideas constantly bubbled to the surface of her thoughts. She could now see major holes in how the company was doing the clinical trials of the drugs. David and the other executives were so busy growing the company that they were missing important opportunities.

As time wore on, Lily began to feel as if her voice had been lost. She had more authority than ever, yet she derived little pleasure from performing tasks she had clearly mastered. She felt disregarded by not being invited to provide more input into the design of clinical trials. She knew she had the skills to do more than run the lab, but she wondered if she would be perceived as unappreciative for saying something about it. For months she remained silent and felt stifled by her job. Things got worse when she realized she was mired in the same frustrating muck she had pulled herself out of just a few years prior. Once again, she was dissatisfied with her work.

Throughout this period, despite her growing melancholy with her job, Lily remained committed to the mentoring and support David offered. He was busier than ever and sometimes a little distant, but he never denied a request to meet. She regretted her failure to voice her frustration. It was time to be honest with David and see if he could help her. She scheduled a meeting with him and had two full weeks in which to prepare.

Deep inside, Lily knew something had to change. She did not want to spend her time stalled in the lab, but she saw no obvious position for her skills in the growing company. Lily decided that getting out of the lab was her first priority. She spent the next two weeks building the courage to explain her experience to David. Whether her feelings were justified or not, she knew he would listen. Whether or not things would actually change was a different story. If David disagreed with her, the possibility of staying sequestered in the lab was not a welcome thought.

During the meeting, Lily sat stiff in her chair. She cleared her throat and nervously explained to David that she had a growing distaste for the limits of her current job. She was quick to point out that she loved the company and appreciated the opportunity, but the last several months had left her feeling stifled. Lily paused for a moment and then told David she wanted to transition out of the lab. Silence fell over the room. For what seemed like an eternity, David did not say a word. He remained in his chair and seemed to look right through her. He was shocked by her revelation and more than a little angry. David felt that Lily held a nice position in a rapidly growing company. She was making double the salary she had at her previous job. He did a pretty good job of hiding his anger, and Lily found it hard to tell what he was thinking.

To break the awkward silence, Lily raised the report she held in her lap and placed it on his desk. Flipping maniacally through the pages, she highlighted the finer points of her analysis of the flaws in the company's current drug trials. She offered her suggestions for improving the trials and explained that these mistakes were costing the company money. She finished by pointing out three weak points that suggested that the company's current trials could fail prematurely. A failed drug trial would cost the company hundreds of thousands of dollars. She could see that David was impressed. After another torturous lull, he made it clear that he had had no idea she was so unhappy with her job. He lamented that the growth of the business had prevented him from checking in with her as much as he would have liked. He also told her that though the report was impressive, he could not promise anything. It was up to the entire executive team to decide if she should transition to a new job overseeing the company's clinical trials of new drugs.

Now it was Lily's turn to look pensive. Did he just say a new position overseeing the company's clinical trials? He had, and later that week he made the recommendation to the rest of the executive team. His suggestion was approved on a probationary basis. Six months later, Lily's squeaky clean efficiency running the trials earned her the title of director and an increase in benefits. The increased compensation and latitude to apply her insights made her feel great. Ironically, the moment in that conversation that stuck with her for years to come was David's comment at the end of the meeting that he admired her courage for trusting her gut and facing the situation directly. This from a guy who had walked away from a $250,000 salary to start a company with his life savings!

Lily later discovered the role emotional intelligence had played in her successful navigation of this difficult situation. She reviewed the experience with an executive coach and explored the specific actions she had taken to get results. Her coach showed her how she had taken advantage of all four emotional intelligence skills: self-awareness, self-management, social awareness, and relationship management. Like most people who explore their emotional intelligence, Lily liked the fact that she could break her emotional intelligence down into four unique parts. Together the four skills define our ability to recognize and understand emotions, as well as our ability to use this awareness to manage our behavior and our relationships. The four-skill model was introduced by Daniel Goleman, Richard Boyatzis, and Annie McKee in their 2002 book *Primal Leadership.* It serves as the benchmark for how people understand and discuss emotional intelligence today, and throughout this book we describe emotional intelligence using these four labels. Like Lily and so many others we've worked with, we're certain you will find it to be an accurate description of the four components of emotional intelligence. Together these skills capture the side of life that typical "smarts" cannot.

Lily used the first emotional intelligence skill, self-awareness, by taking an objective look at her situation. It was painful to realize she was as frustrated and stuck in her new job as she had been at her previous employer. Once she admitted this to herself and took the time to understand her feelings, she had all the information she needed to make a change. Lily then used her awareness of her situation to fuel action. She used the second emotional intelligence skill, self-management, to develop a sound plan and execute it. Evenings sacrificed to work on the report, moments of growing self-doubt, and walking into David's office to face him that day were all challenges she had to overcome by managing her emotions. She fulfilled her strategy by dealing with the negative emotions that surfaced throughout the process and continuing on toward her goal.

Lily took time before the meeting to practice the third emotional intelligence skill, social awareness, and consider how things might look from David's viewpoint. This convinced her to create the report. She realized that he could not see all of the ideas in her head—no matter how compelling they might be—so she created a clear way for him to understand her thinking. She then used the fourth emotional intelligence skill, relationship management, to seal the deal and get results. No one else was going to fix things for her, but she knew David could help. She showed trust in their relationship and went to him directly with her problem.

As Lily compared her actions in this situation to others from her past, she realized the influence her exercise of emotional intelligence had had on the successful outcome. Though she didn't know she was using emotional intelligence skills at the time, staying true to her feelings, doing her homework, and trusting in her relationship with David worked to her benefit. On the flip side, she could think of other opportunities she had missed because she hadn't done the same thing. In discovering her emotional intelligence with the help of her coach, Lily learned ways to identify these skills and magnify them in the future.

The four skills that together make up emotional intelligence. The top two skills, self-awareness and self-management, are more about you. The bottom two skills, social awareness and relationship management, are more about how you are with other people.

A Window on Emotional Intelligence

Descriptions of emotional intelligence are as old as accounts of human behavior. In both testaments of the Bible to the Greek philosophers, Shakespeare, Thomas Jefferson, and modern psychology, the emotional aspect of reason has been discussed as a fundamental element of human nature.[3] People who hone their emotional intelligence have the unique ability to flourish where others flounder. Emotional intelligence is the "something" in each of us that is a bit intangible. It defines how we manage behavior, navigate social complexities, and make personal decisions that achieve positive results.

In the early 1900s, a new movement emerged that sought to measure cognitive intelligence (IQ). Early scientists explored IQ as a quick method of separating average performers from excellent ones. They soon discovered limitations in this approach. Many people were incredibly intelligent (good at reading, writing, and arithmetic) but limited by their ability to manage their behavior and get along well with others. They also found people who excelled in life, despite having average intelligence. E. L. Thorndike, a professor at Columbia University, was the first to give emotional intelligence skills a name. His term "social intelligence" reflected the ability of individuals possessing these skills to get along well with other people.[4] It wasn't until the 1980s that emotional intelligence (EQ) took on its current name.[5] Powerful research soon followed, including a series of studies at Yale University that linked emotional intelligence to personal achievement, happiness, and professional success.[6]

The concept of emotional intelligence explained why two people of the same IQ can attain vastly different levels of success in life. Emotional intelligence taps into a fundamental element of human behavior that is distinct from your intellect. There is no known connection between IQ and EQ; you simply can't predict emotional intelligence based on how smart someone is. This is great news because cognitive intelligence, or IQ, is not flexible. Your IQ, short of a traumatic event such as a brain injury, is fixed from birth. You don't get smarter by learning new facts or information. Intelligence is your *ability* to learn, and it's the same at age fifteen as it is at age fifty. Emotional intelligence, on the other hand, is a flexible skill that is readily learned. While it is true that some people are naturally more emotionally intelligent than others, a high EQ can be developed even if you aren't born with it.

Personality is the final piece in the puzzle. It's the "style" that defines each of us. Your personality is a result of your preferences, such as your inclination to introversion or extroversion. But like IQ, personality

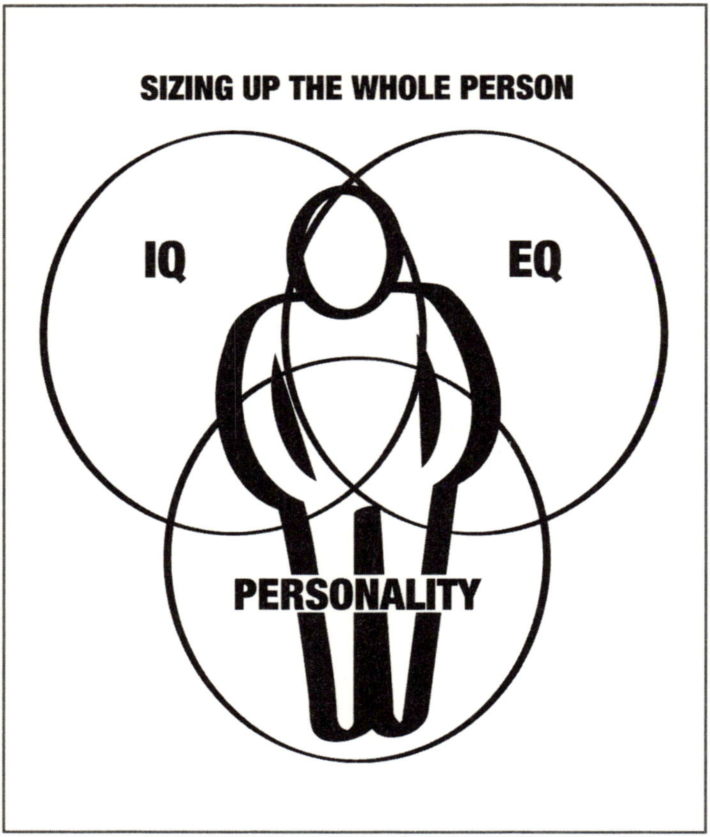

Intelligence (IQ), personality, and emotional intelligence (EQ) are distinct qualities we all possess. Together they determine how we think and act. It is impossible to predict one based upon another. People may be intelligent but not emotionally intelligent, and people of all types of personalities can be high in EQ and/or IQ. Of the three, emotional intelligence is the only quality that is flexible and able to change.

can't be used to predict emotional intelligence. Also like IQ, personality is stable over a lifetime. Personality traits appear early in life, and they don't go away. People often assume that certain traits (for example, extroversion) are associated with a higher emotional intelligence, but those who prefer to be with other people are no more emotionally intelligent than people who prefer to be alone. You can use your personality to assist in developing your emotional intelligence, but the latter isn't dependent on the former. Emotional intelligence is a flexible skill, while personality does not change. IQ, EQ, and personality, assessed together, are the best ways to get a picture of the whole person. When all three are measured in a single individual, they don't overlap much. Instead, each covers unique ground that helps to explain what makes a person tick.

The four emotional intelligence skills tend to pair up under two primary competencies: personal competence and social competence. Personal competence is a result of your self-awareness and self-management skills. It's your ability to stay aware of your emotions and manage your behavior and tendencies. Social competence is a result of your social awareness and relationship management skills. It's your ability to understand other people's behavior and motives and manage your relationships.[7] The skills that pair up to form personal and social competence occur together so often that they don't even show up independently in a statistical analysis. You will see that you often use these emotional intelligence skills in tandem. Just like Lily, you will become aware of situations in which a single skill is not enough to get the desired results. Our experience confirms what countless astute audience members have whispered to us after a talk: "Don't some of these emotional intelligence skills just end up together?"

Personal Competence

Personal competence is the product of your ability in two important skills, self-awareness and self-management. These skills focus more on you individually than on your interactions with other people. Self-awareness is your ability to accurately perceive your own emotions in the moment and understand your tendencies across situations. Self-awareness includes staying on top of your typical reactions to specific events, challenges, and even people. A keen understanding of your tendencies is important; it facilitates your ability to quickly make sense of your emotions. A high degree of self-awareness requires a willingness to tolerate the discomfort of focusing directly on feelings that may be negative. It is essential to address and understand your positive emotions as well.

The only way to genuinely understand your emotions is to spend enough time thinking through them to figure out where they are coming from and why they are there. Emotions always serve a purpose. Because they are reactions to your life experience, they always come from somewhere. Many times they seem to arise out of thin air, and it's important to understand why your current circumstances are important enough to generate a certain reaction in you. People who do this can often cut to the core of a feeling very quickly. Situations that create strong emotions will always require more thought. It was hard for Lily to admit that her new job had turned sour. It took her weeks to realize that she was frustrated that the new job was mirroring the old. This prolonged period of reflection paved the way for a constructive change and prevented her from choosing a path that was destructive to her career.

Self-management is what happens when you act—or do not act. It is dependent on your self-awareness and is the second major piece of personal competence. Self-management is your ability to use your awareness of your emotions to stay flexible and direct your behavior positively. This means managing your emotional reactions to situations and people. Some emotions create a paralyzing fear that makes your thinking so cloudy that the best course of action is nowhere to be found—assuming that there is something you should be doing. In such circumstances self-management is revealed by your ability to tolerate an exploration of your emotions. Once you understand and build comfort with the breadth of your feelings, the best course of action will show itself.

Social Competence

Social competence focuses on your ability to understand other people and manage relationships. It is the product of the emotional intelligence skills that come to life in the presence of others: social awareness and relationship management. Social awareness is your ability to accurately pick up on emotions in other people and understand what is really going on with them. This often means perceiving what other people are thinking and feeling even if you do not feel the same way. It's easy to get so caught up in your own emotions that you forget to consider the perspective of the other party. Despite Lily's frustration, she used social awareness by taking the time to consider what things must look like from David's chair. Regardless of who was right or wrong, she picked up on his anger and confusion early in the meeting and went right to what she knew would appeal to him: the data she had assembled. Her social awareness opened the door to a successful meeting.

Relationship management is the product of the first three emotional intelligence skills: self-

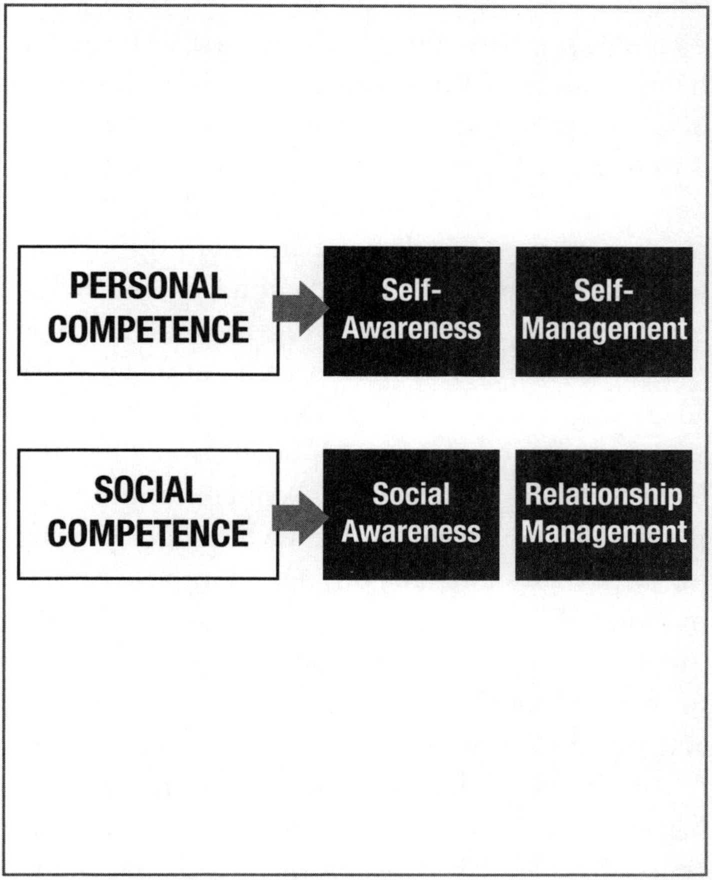

Emotional intelligence is the product of two main skills: personal and social competence. Personal competence focuses more on you as an individual, and is divided into self-awareness and self-management. Social competence focuses more on how you behave with other people, and is divided into social awareness and relationship management.

awareness, self-management, and social awareness. It's your ability to use your awareness of both your own emotions and those of others to manage interactions successfully. This ensures clear communication and effective handling of conflict. In Lily's meeting, she managed the relationship through her response to David's anger and confusion over her request. She kept things moving forward and controlled the discomfort that so many of us feel when addressing a superior. Relationship management is also the bond you build with others over time. People who manage relationships well are committed to their value and are able to see the benefit of connecting with many different people, even those they are not fond of. Solid relationships are a commodity that should be sought and cherished. They are the result of how you understand people, how you treat them, and the history you share.

Lily's story illustrates the good things that can happen when you focus on your emotional intelligence. Her coworkers were surprised by her sudden promotion and admired her courage in creating the opportunity. The depiction of Phineas Gage is an example of a life devoid of emotional intelligence. For the eleven years he survived after the accident, people marveled at the amazing man who was living with a "hole in the head," but they did so from a lonely distance.

The Discovery

After Phineas died, his headless body was buried in San Francisco's Lone Mountain Cemetery and lay there undisturbed for a hundred years. His skull and the tamping iron that traveled through it were placed on display at the Harvard Medical School. In 1940, growing pains in the San Francisco area pressured city officials to move the bodies from the cemetery to create room for housing. The tombstones were dumped into the bay to create a breakwater. Every February since—the same month in which he fell terminally ill—the tombstones have risen from the sand along the beach, exposed by low tide and winter erosion. Among them, a solitary stone bears the name of Phineas Gage. Like his life, it continues to surface as an eerie reminder of the power of emotional intelligence.

Chapter 2

AMAZING EQ

HALF A MILLION SURVEYS

WHAT DO THEY TEACH US ABOUT THE NEED FOR EMOTIONAL INTELLIGENCE?

◆

Emotions have taught mankind to reason.

LUC DE VAUVENARGUES

Racing through downtown traffic on a motor scooter is no way to start the day. Louis Sullivan was late for work and dodging between cars like a madman. As if this weren't uncomfortable enough, it was already 100 degrees outside. A red light forced him to stop, and he could feel the oppressive heat radiating from the blacktop through the bottoms of his loafers. The scooter had always been a useful tool when he was running late for work, but today he cursed it. When he pulled up to his building, he couldn't even find a scooter-sized place to park in. "Desperate times call for desperate measures," he muttered under his breath as he slammed down the kickstand. He tilted the scooter to rest on the edge of a disabled parking spot in front of the building and scuttled inside.

The sweat was already pouring through his shirt when he plopped down at his desk, anticipating another uneventful day. He quickly lost himself in e-mails and phone calls, and the lunch hour was fast approaching when a coworker leaned over the edge of his cubicle. "There's a tow truck out front, and he's taking your scooter!" Louis leapt from his chair and stormed through the lobby. The sticky August heat was a familiar greeting as he thrust the front doors open and stepped out onto the sidewalk. Sure enough a bearded man in a navy jumpsuit was kneeling next to his scooter, searching for the proper place to attach it so he could lift it onto the tow truck. Louis rushed over and begged for his forgiveness.

"No can do, my friend," the driver interrupted. "This is a tow-away zone."

"You don't need to tow it if I'm here to move it," Louis pleaded to a blank stare.

"Rule's a rule. I'm just trying to do my job." The driver sighed and went back to looking underneath the scooter.

Louis's mind flooded with confusion and despair. Getting his scooter out of tow would cost more money than he had earned that week. He could scarcely afford his rent as it was.

"Come on, man! Can't you see I'm desperate?"

The driver glanced up for a moment to greet this comment with a smirk. Tunnel vision set in, and Louis could now see the crumbs in the driver's beard, probably left over from some seafood special. Of course, he's already had lunch. Louis thought to himself. Why would he have to wait until noon like the rest of us? He jammed his hands into his pockets and glanced back at the growing assembly of his coworkers gathered in front of the building to witness the debacle.

"Why can't I just pay the fine and keep my scooter?" Louis demanded.

This time the driver began to chuckle. He stood

up and faced Louis to make his point clear. "You just don't get it, do you buddy?" He extended his left index finger toward the offending vehicle and continued, "Your little scooter here is parked in a handicapped spot, and they called me here to tow it away. I'll be damned if I'm gonna leave without it."

Now Louis was seeing red. He'd had enough. He lurched to his left and with all his might planted a foot into the passenger side door of the tow truck. After pausing for a moment to admire the size 11 dent his shoe had left in the metal, he turned to gauge the owner's reaction. The man was standing there laughing. He raised his hand and pointed to the police cruiser parked on the corner. Louis's blood ran cold. It was the police who had called for a tow, and they were still there, unnoticed by him. The cops fired up their siren and screeched to a halt in front of Louis. He was so shocked by what was happening that they seemed to come at him in slow motion. Many of Louis's coworkers, including his boss, watched in silence as the police cuffed him, read him his rights, and then ducked him into the back of the squad car. When his girlfriend bailed him out of jail that evening, she had all of his belongings in the trunk of her Hyundai. As if getting arrested and fired in a single day weren't bad enough, she broke up with him immediately as a result of his irrational behavior.

Louis's difficulty understanding and controlling his emotions, though dramatic, is not uncommon. People overrun by intense emotions often make difficult situations worse. Over the last decade we've tested more than 500,000 people to explore the role emotions play in daily living and learn what works and what doesn't in the face of challenges. The results are astounding. Our database contains 25 million answers to the most critical questions facing people today. We've learned how people see themselves versus what others see in them, and we've observed how various choices affect personal and professional success. Our findings pinpoint three simple truths that capture the essence of emotional intelligence.

Finding 1: We Have an Emotional Epidemic

Despite the growing focus on emotions and emotional intelligence during the last two decades, the global deficit in understanding and managing emotions is startling. Only 36 percent of the people we tested are able to accurately identify their emotions as they happen. This means that two thirds of us are typically controlled by our emotions and are not yet skilled at spotting them and using them to our benefit. Emotional awareness and understanding are not taught in school. We enter the workforce knowing how to read, write, and report on bodies of knowledge, but too often we lack the skills to manage our emotions in the heat of the challenging problems we will face. Good decisions require far more than factual knowledge. They are made using self-knowledge and emotional mastery when they're needed most.

Stress and interpersonal conflict are glaring evidence of the trouble most people have understanding and managing their emotions. More than 70 percent of those we tested have difficulty handling stress, and some of the most challenging circumstances they face are at work. Conflicts at work tend to fester as people passively avoid problems or confront them so aggressively that situations are blown out of proportion. Most organizations perpetuate an environment that stifles emotional intelligence. They lose sight of the very people who keep the dollars coming in. Only 15 percent of workers we surveyed feel strongly that they are respected and valued by their employer. Four out of every five people would be likely to leave their current job if offered similar pay and position elsewhere. People want more than a paycheck for coming to work: they want to know that their efforts are valued and the sacrifices they make for their employer are appreciated.

Finding 2: There Are Few Truths Behind Labels

Gender is a common framework for assigning labels to emotion. Such generalizations have pegged women as everything from "the fairer sex" to "overly emotional" and men from "emotionally aloof" to "explosive."[1] Our analysis of emotional intelligence by gender suggests something different. Women, on average, have an overall emotional intelligence score that is four points higher than men's. This difference is large enough to suggest that women typically express (not to be confused with possess) more skill in using emotions to their benefit. Women outscore men in three of the four emotional intelligence skills, including self-management, social awareness, and relationship management. Self-awareness is the only skill for which the scores are equal by gender. The largest gap occurs in relationship management, with women scoring a full 10 points higher than men. One thing data can't provide is interpretation. We imagine that women are expected to practice emotional intelligence from childhood. Many of the pretend games young girls play involve acting out feelings and social niceties. Boys aren't rewarded for the same behavior.

People often assume that there are vast differences in emotional intelligence between members of different professions. Engineers, accountants, and scientists are often believed to have a low emotional intelligence. But analysis of our global database produces dramatic, counterintuitive findings. First, there is essentially no difference among the average scores of various professions. Persons working in fields as diverse as sales, IT, finance, operations, and marketing have an average emotional intelligence score that is nearly identical. The gap in emotional intelligence scores among these professions is less than one point. The only group of people who tend to score higher than others are those working in customer service. It appears that a slightly higher level of emotional intelligence is required to survive in this profession. Consider what it's like to deal with disgruntled customers all day long, and you'll see why emotional intelligence is essential. The only group that scores a great deal lower than the other professions is the group whose members have no profession at all: the unemployed.

Finding 3: It's Lonely at the Top

The relationship between emotional intelligence and job title is the most dramatic. Scores climb with titles, from the bottom of the corporate ladder upward toward middle management. Middle managers stand out, with the highest emotional intelligence scores in the workforce. But up beyond middle management, there is a steep downward trend in emotional intelligence scores. For the titles of director and above, scores descend faster than a skier on a black diamond. CEOs, on average, have the lowest emotional intelligence scores.

Business journals often say that the higher your job title, the less real work you do; your primary function is to get work done by other people. You might think, then, that the higher the position, the better the people skills. It appears that the opposite is true. Too many leaders are promoted because of what they know or how long they have worked, rather than for their skill in managing others. Once they reach the top, they actually spend less time interacting with staff. Yet among executives, those with the highest emotional intelligence scores are the best performers. We've found that emotional intelligence skills are more important to job performance than any other leadership skill. The same holds true for every job title: those with the highest emotional intelligence scores within any position outperform their peers.

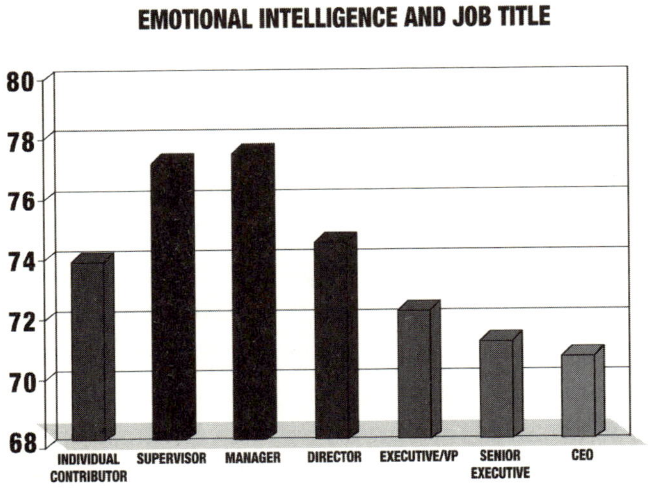

The chart above represents our findings of average emotional intelligence scores for different job titles. The sharp decline for director titles and above reveals the incredible deficit in emotional intelligence among senior leadership in organizations. For every title above, emotional intelligence has more influence on job performance than any other skill.

The Impact of Emotional Intelligence

HOW DOES EMOTIONAL INTELLIGENCE AFFECT YOUR HEALTH AND HAPPINESS?

◆

Even a blind pig in a blizzard finds an acorn once in a while.

ANONYMOUS

The public knew from day one that making *The Magic Hour* a hit was going to be a challenge. Magic Johnson, though an eminently popular celebrity, had made his thirteen-year career with the Los Angeles Lakers legendary by sinking stylish layups at the buzzer, not making jokes on television. The public knew it; the executives at Fox knew it; even Magic Johnson knew it.

A rarely mentioned element of late-night talk shows is the support staff of comedians, who provide the secret ingredient of success. Craig Shoemaker was beaming when he was offered this job on the new show to feature Magic Johnson. Telling jokes with

Magic sounded a heck of a lot better than the gig he had on a game show, and he promptly quit. When he joined the planning for the production, he was told he would sit next to Magic on the couch feeding and receiving lines to keep things lively. And why shouldn't he? Craig had been voted "Best Stand-up" at the 1997 American Comedy Awards, had hosted a program on VH1, and was considered a premier comedian by many in the business. The producers figured that a single day of rehearsal before shooting would be enough time for Magic and Craig to build chemistry. It wasn't. Shoemaker worried that their lack of preparation was a recipe for disaster. He made the most of the single rehearsal and developed some chemistry with Magic during unscripted moments. He remained both optimistic and apprehensive about the show's launch.

The Magic Hour premiered on June 8, 1999, to subpar Nielsen ratings.[2] To Craig's horror, he was handed a list of jokes and instructed to deliver them on cue. With all opportunity for spontaneity pulled out from under him, his bits were painful and the show garnered horrendous reviews. Craig worked hard between episodes to create funny jokes and skits that the producers would let him use on air. He clung to the hope of redeeming himself, but his attempts were repeatedly ignored. The scripted, crude jokes embarrassed him, and his hope quickly morphed into frustration. Craig never mustered the courage to jump ship, and shooting the next fifteen episodes was "an absolute nightmare."

Today Craig is the first to admit that he was afraid to follow his gut. His excitement over the initial opportunity with the program made him immune to the warning signs staring him in the face. He told himself that things would change and waited for them to improve. They didn't. Even Magic Johnson, the "King of the Assist" in the NBA, couldn't save Craig from the atrocious humor he had to read from the script. Craig describes his remaining time on set like being in a jet that has suddenly lost cabin pressure at thirty thousand feet: "The jokes they had me telling were so bad, there should have been oxygen masks falling out of the ceiling for the audience members. It was absolutely terrible."[3] Just weeks into the job, he knew he should bail out, but he felt too paralyzed to walk away.

A $10 million loss forced Fox executives to pull the plug on the program after just eight weeks.[4] Craig's time spent on *The Magic Hour* put a noticeable dent in his career. "I was hoping to have that job title removed from my résumé," he joked recently during a radio interview. "They called me everything from cohost to sidekick to writer to 'You're outta here.'" Always the comedian, he can laugh about it now, but the progress he's made in the seven years since the show ended was slow to start. A comedian fired from a bad show is not a hot commodity in Hollywood. He has since returned successfully to television and is, thankfully, a lot wiser about his feelings. He knows he'll be courageous and trust his gut the next time he sees the writing on the wall.

Emotional Intelligence and Health

There is a time in the life of every predicament where it is ripe for resolution. Your emotions provide you with the cue to act when a problem is big enough to see, yet still small enough to solve. By understanding your emotions, you can move adeptly through your current challenges and prevent future ones. When you do the opposite and repress your feelings, they quickly build into the uncomfortable sensations of tension, stress, and anxiety. Unaddressed emotions strain the mind and body. Your emotional intelligence skills help make stress more manageable by enabling you to tackle tough situations before they become unmanageable. People who fail to use their emotional intelligence skills are more likely to turn to other, less effective means of managing their moods. They are twice as likely to experience anxiety, depression, substance abuse, and even thoughts of suicide.[5] Emotional intelligence has a tremendous impact on people's happiness and contentment. People who practice emotional intelligence tend to be more at ease with their surroundings and comfortable in their own skin.[6] The direct connection between emotional intelligence and a sense of well-being underscores how critical it is that we notice our emotions, remain aware of them, and use them to guide our behavior. The more you exercise your emotional intelligence skills, the more you will get out of life.

Scores of recent research studies have indicated an important link between emotional intelligence and susceptibility to disease. Stress, anxiety, and depression suppress the immune system, creating a vulnerability to everything from the common cold to cancer.[7] The potency of your immune system is tied to your emotional state via neuropeptides, complex chemicals that act as messengers between the mind and body. When your mind is flooded with tension or distress, it signals the body to decrease the energy it expends to fight disease. This increases your vulnerability to illness, and medical schools and continuing education programs for physicians are rushing to add this discovery to their curricula.[8]

New medical research shows a definitive link between emotional distress and serious forms of illness, such as cancer.[9] One of the first long-term studies measured women's stress levels from 1968 to 1991.

Researchers tracked the degree to which each woman experienced tension, fear, anxiety, and sleep disturbances, all resulting from conflicts at work and home. Women who experienced higher levels of stress during this twenty-four-year period were twice as likely to develop breast cancer.[10] The emotional distress these women experienced resulted from unresolved conflicts and unmanaged emotions.

Emotional intelligence skills can also help speed the body's recovery from disease. People who develop their emotional intelligence skills during treatment recover faster from a variety of ailments, including the two biggest killers in America, heart disease and cancer.[11] Teaching emotional intelligence skills to people with life-threatening illnesses has been shown to reduce their rate of recurrence, lessen recovery times, and lower death rates.[12] When individuals are diagnosed with a life-threatening illness such as cancer, they often feel an increase in stress and anxiety in response to the diagnosis. The illness is usually the biggest challenge the patient has ever faced, and she often needs new skills to cope with the associated stress and uncertainty. For example, a third of all women diagnosed with breast cancer suffer a bout of clinically diagnosable anxiety upon diagnosis, and up to 10 percent suffer from posttraumatic stress. Researchers at Ohio State University studied 227 women diagnosed with breast cancer and saw remarkable effects from teaching emotional intelligence skills during recovery.[13] Women who were randomly assigned to this treatment had reduced levels of stress, kept to a better diet, and developed stronger immune systems. Research presented to the American Heart Association revealed a similar outcome for men and women taught emotional intelligence skills while recovering from a heart attack.[14]

Emotional intelligence has a strong influence on health-related outcomes because it reduces stress in the face of trying situations. Life-threatening illnesses, in particular, arouse intense fear and apprehension that must be addressed and understood by the patient for his benefit. The physical impact of emotional intelligence is so strong that studies at the Harvard Medical School have actually mapped physical differences in the brain based on changes in emotional intelligence. In these studies, the amount of "traffic" flowing between the rational and emotional centers of the brain was found to have a real impact on their size and structure.[15] Emotional intelligence skills strengthen your brain's ability to cope with emotional distress. This resilience keeps your immune system strong and helps protect you from disease.

Emotional Intelligence and Professional Excellence

How much impact does the exercise of emotional intelligence have on professional success? The short answer is: *a lot!* It's a powerful way to focus your energy in one direction with a tremendous result. We've tested emotional intelligence alongside thirty-three other important workplace behaviors and found that it subsumes the majority of them, including time management, motivation, vision, and communication. You can use your emotional intelligence to boost your job performance in a variety of ways. It's so critical to success that it accounts for 60 percent of performance in all types of jobs. It's the single biggest predictor of performance in the workplace and the strongest driver of leadership and personal excellence.

Perhaps the best thing about emotional intelligence is that it's a highly flexible skill. No matter whether people measure high or low in this ability, they can work to improve it, and those who score low can actually catch up to their coworkers. Research conducted at the business school at the University of Queensland in Australia discovered that people who are low in emotional intelligence and job performance can match their colleagues who excel in both—solely by working to improve their emotional intelligence.[16] Of all the people we've studied at work, we have found that 90 percent of high performers are also high in emotional intelligence. On the flip side, just 20 percent of low performers are high in emotional intelligence. You can be a high performer without emotional intelligence, but the chances are slim. People who develop their emotional intelligence tend to be successful on the job because the two go hand in hand. These findings hold true for people in all industries, at all levels, in every region of the world. We haven't yet been able to find a job in which performance isn't tied to emotional intelligence.

Organizations as a whole also benefit from emotional intelligence. When the skills of thousands of people in a single company are increased, the business itself leaps forward. Emotional intelligence skills drive leadership, teamwork, and customer service. Organizations as varied as L'Oréal and the U.S. Air Force have saved millions of dollars by instituting programs targeting emotional intelligence skills.[17] We often see a contagious frenzy when companies introduce emotional intelligence to employees. One of our Fortune 500 clients posted an offer on its intranet inviting employees to test their emotional intelligence and complete a training program online. People in human resources were floored when they received hundreds of responses each day. The emotional intelligence program became a word-of-mouth phenomenon. Let's face it, training programs can be pretty boring. Too many times employees attend programs they consider nothing more than a nuisance. If a company can generate contagious energy around a single concept, it fuels a culture in which people can thrive. When people build their emotional intelligence, they perform better, treat one another better, and get more out of going to work. It helps create an environment in which everybody wins.

TWO

Discover Your Emotional Intelligence

Chapter 3

THE EMOTIONAL INTELLIGENCE APPRAISAL

TESTING FOR EMOTIONAL INTELLIGENCE

◆

We must not cease from exploration. And the end of all our exploring will be to arrive where we began and know the place for the first time.

T. S. ELIOT

When you test people for emotional intelligence, you quickly learn that they tend to take their results very seriously. When people take most tests that measure something other than intelligence—a personality test is a good example—they can feel good about the results no matter where they stand. An emotional intelligence test is another story. When we share with someone how "emotionally intelligent" she is, it can be a threatening experience. Even a skeptical executive who just heard the term for the first time that morning knows that a low score is trouble. This concern is well founded. An ample body of research worldwide demonstrates that emotional intelligence is critical to success both at work and at home.

Why create a test that seems to put a "box" around someone's emotional intelligence? Mostly because people want to know. Emotional intelligence is drawing a tremendous amount of attention around the globe because it hits home and is real for people. It's easy to understand why emotional intelligence is important: human beings were made to feel. More people search for emotional intelligence on the Internet than they do for John Travolta, *The Tonight Show*, or flat-screen televisions. The TalentSmart.com Web site alone receives more than a hundred thousand hits each month from visitors who are seeking to learn more about emotional intelligence. We all have some idea of how we come across to other people, but even the least self-aware among us realizes that self-perception is generally tainted by how we want things to be. An emotional intelligence test provides an objective evaluation of behavior. It shows how we come across to other people and how we handle the situations that matter most.

Measuring your emotional intelligence moves your learning beyond a factual or motivational exercise. When you know your score, the experience of developing emotional intelligence is more real, relevant, and personal. The value of testing your emotional intelligence is akin to learning the waltz with an actual partner. If I tell you how the dance works, you are likely to learn something and may even get the urge to try it yourself. If, as I show you how to do a waltz, you practice each step with a partner, your chances of remembering them later on the dance floor go up exponentially. The emotional intelligence profile you receive from taking the test is your dance partner in developing these skills. It will remind you where to step with every beat of the music.

As you read this book and move beyond it to develop new skills, it helps to reflect on where your emotional intelligence "stands" and which skills you need most. No test can determine this for you, but your profile will help you understand your strengths as well as the skills that will provide you with the greatest opportunity for improvement. If you take the Emotional Intelligence Appraisal that comes with this book, you will expand your knowledge of your ability to understand emotions and your tendencies with different situations and people. There will likely be a few surprises in your profile. Some may sting a little, but everything you will learn is to your benefit. Your results will increase your self-awareness and open the door to change.

The Emotional Intelligence Appraisal

HOW DOES IT WORK, AND HOW DO I COMPLETE IT?

◆

The greatest of faults is to be conscious of none.

THOMAS CARLYLE

The first thing most people notice when taking the Emotional Intelligence Appraisal is that it's very fast. The average time required to complete it is just seven minutes. We have been both praised and scolded for the length of this test and are happy to report that its speed does not mean it's a *Cosmo* quiz. Your scores in each of the four emotional intelligence skills are accurately measured by your answers to just 28 questions. We could add more questions to please the critics (who believe a psychological test *must* have at least 100 questions), but they would just be filler. Years of research have revealed that the test is the optimal length to measure your emotional intelligence without wasting your time.

Do I Have to Take the Emotional Intelligence Appraisal?

Absolutely not. The emotional intelligence strategies discussed in this book are not dependent upon your knowing your emotional intelligence score. While the test provides additional insight into your emotional intelligence skills, you can easily develop them without taking the test. The test is provided to deliver a new, objective perspective of your behavior. It can be used as a supplement to what you learn in this book, but by no means is it required for you to be able to reap the benefits of what you read.

If I Take the Test, What Will It Tell Me?

First and foremost, the test will tell you which skills are your strengths and which areas can use improvement. You will learn more about your tendencies and behavior than you could on your own. Your profile will provide an overall emotional intelligence score, scores for personal and social competence, and scores in each of the four emotional intelligence skills—self-awareness, self-management, social awareness, and relationship management. The results highlight specific actions that are most critical to increasing your emotional intelligence. In your online report you will see a specific analysis of the behaviors that contributed to your results. Each skill is further illustrated through e-learning activities that bring emotional intelligence to life via clips from Hollywood movies, television, and real-world events. A goal-tracking system summarizes the skills you are working on and provides automatic reminders via e-mail to help you stay focused.

You will also learn how your scores compare to other people's. You will see what percentage of the population you scored higher than and how your scores compare to those of specific groups with which you share certain characteristics. You can "ask" your report to contrast your scores with others based on gender, region of the world, job type, and job title. For example, you might discover how you compare to other women in their forties who hold a vice president of sales title at a company in North America.

How Do I Take the Test?

It's simple: Take the dust jacket off your book, and you will find a code printed on the reverse side. You will see a unique ID code printed there specifically for you. Write the code down somewhere, put the jacket back on the book, and hop onto a computer with Internet access. Visit the page www.eiquickbook.com to take your test. Click the gray button in the middle of the page that says "I'm ready." When the system asks for your ID code, you will need to type in the code from the inside of your book jacket. You can type the letters in capital or lowercase; it does not matter. (To complete the test, you will need a computer with Internet access, a web browser, and a 28.8-kbps or faster modem.)

Very few people find the test questions difficult or stressful to complete. Since the test asks simple questions about your behavior, you already have all the answers. Follow the instructions on the page and think about how you are in many situations, not just the ones you handle well. When you complete the test, it will instantly create your score profile. You will see your results immediately and can return to view them anytime. The system will also let you print your results and save them as a document on your computer. How much time you spend reviewing your score profile and participating in the online activities is up to you. Some people spend just ten or twenty minutes reading through their results. Others spend more time, using the related activities available.

Chapter 4

IMPORTANT QUESTIONS

SEVEN KEY QUESTIONS

GETTING STARTED

◆

The end of understanding is not to prove and find reasons, but to know and believe.

THOMAS CARLYLE

We find the people who make the most progress in improving their emotional intelligence are usually the ones who ask the most questions. A question is the child of curiosity, and topics that can generate this level of interest are worthy of exploration. Too often, questions are viewed as a sign of doubt and lack of faith in the subject of the inquisition. We realize that challenging questions come from a desire to know more. To this end we have tracked the seven most common inquiries about emotional intelligence, and the answers follow.

Can My Emotional Intelligence Change?

Emotional intelligence skills change as you do. Unlike regular intelligence and personality, your emotional intelligence is a flexible skill that you can choose to improve. It is also influenced by significant life circumstances. You may see it fluctuate in response to losing a job, getting a divorce, being promoted unexpectedly, or other major life events. The real trick is to understand your emotional intelligence skills, keep an eye on them, and use them to your benefit. Your scores on the test included with this book should not be treated as the final verdict on your emotional intelligence skills. Instead, use them to see where you stand today.

They will help you know if you are headed in the right direction. The more you work to hone your emotional intelligence skills, the more you will find your scores ending up where you want them to be.

When you work to improve your emotional intelligence, it will take a few months to begin seeing a lasting change. Learning to pause during your day and think differently in response to your surroundings is all it takes to get started. Some new behaviors are easy to initiate quickly, and people will notice the change in you immediately. Shifting your focus to emotional intelligence can give you a new perspective that will make it hard not to change. Like learning any new skill, improving your emotional intelligence takes practice, and most people see a measurable change three to six months after they start working on a new skill. After you spend a few months putting the skills you'll learn in chapters 5 to 8 into practice, it's a good idea to test your emotional intelligence again to see where your scores improved.

If Emotional Intelligence Is So Important, Why Are Some People Successful Who Seem to Have None?

Just about every office has someone who meets this description. He doesn't get along well with other people. Most conversations begin with tension and easily end in some type of conflict. Approaching him with a question is about as comfortable as listening to someone drag his or her fingernails down a chalkboard. Yet somehow this person is good at getting things done. Many of these people are leaders who are particularly abrasive with those who work for them. The first thing to realize is that emotional intelligence and success do not *always* occur together. People can use their intellect to get results without being successful in dealing with other people, but in failing to use social competence they don't realize their full potential.

When you work with people like this, it's easy to lose sight of the fact that they succeed through personal competence. Many of the same people who are bristly to speak to are really good at motivating themselves to get work done. They may not manage their behavior with other people well, but they can power through a dreary task. It's a side of emotional intelligence that is private, yet it's only one side; these folks typically have a low overall emotional intelligence score. It's important to understand that the success they've obtained has been enabled by a certain level of self-management and likely a good deal of intellect. Difficult people who achieve a lot are in the minority, however; about 90 percent of top performers are high in emotional intelligence.

How Many Emotional Intelligence Skills Should I Work on at One Time?

The human mind can focus effectively on only a few behaviors at a time. An attempt to improve all four emotional intelligence skills in a single effort are bound to fail. You should work on one emotional intelligence skill at a time; that will require you to focus on changing a few key behaviors to get results. As an example, if you choose to work on self-management you should not spend your time thinking, "I need to self-manage . . . I need to self-manage." Rather, you need to hatch a plan that incorporates specific actions into your routine. You might make an effort to consider multiple options before reaching decisions, or you might try not to brush people off when you're having a bad day. Each of these behaviors is a significant new challenge. Only once you've mastered them should you move on to something new.

It's also important to remember that the four emotional intelligence skills have a good deal of overlap with one another. If you begin working on self-management, your other skills are likely to improve as well. Citing the example from the paragraph above, you clearly have to self-manage in order to learn not to brush people off when something is bothering you. This will also improve your relationships, increasing your relationship management score. You also might find along the way that focusing on other people's perspective makes it easier to avoid brushing them off. Doing so will create an improvement in your social awareness. So even the most ambitious people should trust that working diligently on a single skill will take you far. The four emotional intelligence skills will work together for your benefit.

Should I Let Other People Know That I Am Working on My Emotional Intelligence?

If you feel comfortable doing so, you should share your goals with at least one person you trust. If that person is even the least bit supportive, you will find that he or she is a boon to your efforts. When you make a goal public—even by simply telling someone else what you're working on—you are ten times more likely to achieve that goal.[1] Just putting it out there creates a new level of accountability. Other people will also be an important source of information as you monitor your progress. They can describe how they see your efforts taking effect. There are some people whom you may not want to tell, and this is usually for the best. In order for you to benefit from sharing your goals with another person, that person has to be willing to engage in a comfortable and constructive collaboration. If the person you tell isn't going to take the time to understand or is just going to give you a hard time about it, you are better off working on your emotional intelligence goals privately.

If you take the Emotional Intelligence Appraisal, your scores will be protected and we will not show them to anyone, under any circumstances. Your ability to access them will be password-protected, ensuring that another person using your computer will not be able to see them. We believe that personal development should be as private as you want it to be. From time to time, qualified behavioral scientists from TalentSmart do conduct research on the anonymous database. They are bound to the ethical standards required of those trained in this profession and see only blocks of numbers without identifying information.

Can Emotional Intelligence Be Used to Manipulate People?

Yes. The power of emotional intelligence is not lost on those who use these skills to manipulate others. Unfortunately, there is nothing to stop people from using emotional intelligence for ill gain. A prime example of someone using emotional intelligence to manipulate another occurs in the movie *Catch Me If You Can,* starring Leonardo DiCaprio and Tom Hanks. The movie is a true story based on the life of Frank Abignale—played by DiCaprio—a successful young check counterfeiter who has attracted the attention of the FBI. Hanks plays an FBI agent, Carl Hanratty, who has tracked the counterfeiter to a Los Angeles hotel room without a clue as to what he looks like.

When Agent Hanratty enters the room with his gun drawn, he finds a man who claims to be a CIA agent. Hanratty aggressively questions the man without lowering his gun. The impostor searches the room, explaining that the CIA has long been on the case and that Agent Hanratty is too late—the fugitive is already on the run. But the "CIA agent" is really the fugitive, and he eventually convinces Hanratty of his story. He uses a couple of tricks along the way, but his success ultimately comes from maintaining a calm demeanor. He's so good at managing his anxiety about getting caught that he appears relaxed and calm. Hanratty assumes that there is no way he could be the fugitive and eventually lets his guard down. Abignale escapes when Agent Hanratty lets him walk out of the room to carry some "evidence" to his car. In real life, emotional intelligence helped Frank Abignale narrowly escape the clutches of the FBI.

Does Emotional Intelligence Have Anything to Do with Age?

Emotional intelligence scores tend to increase with age. Most people increase in self-awareness throughout their lifetime and have an easier time managing their emotions and behavior as they age. People in their fifties, on average, score 25 percent higher on our test than those in their twenties. Most people tend to gain a few emotional intelligence points with every decade of life. While there is a natural increase in emotional intelligence for most people as they age, the key is to maximize your emotional intelligence at *every* age. In a matter of months, you can realize an increase in your emotional intelligence that might not otherwise happen for a decade.

Can I Give My Kids the Emotional Intelligence Appraisal?

The Emotional Intelligence Appraisal test questions are written for anyone with the equivalent of an eighth-grade education. The test scores will be descriptive only for those who can read at this level. Younger children, regardless of reading level, typically lack the maturity needed to benefit from an emotional intelligence test. The results are reliable in a variety of settings. You don't need to hold a job to measure your emotional intelligence. For example, we are aware of many high school teachers and university professors who have their students take the test as part of a self-development process to understand their capabilities outside of regular intelligence.

THREE

How to Increase Your Emotional Intelligence

Chapter 5

CHANGING YOUR MIND

YOUR BRAIN IS PLASTIC

CAN I REALLY CHANGE MY BRAIN?

◆

Human beings, by changing the inner attitudes of their minds, can change the outer aspects of their lives.

WILLIAM JAMES

I met Richard La China in such an unremarkable way. He came by our office one Friday to work on our computer network, representing a company referred by a friend. When it was my computer's turn to get fixed, I moved to the couch in my office so he could get to work. As he punched away on the keyboard, he eyed a Ken Blanchard book that had made its way to my floor. He told me he was a Blanchard fan and had read all of Ken's books. As most of my current projects end up on the floor, I enthusiastically explained that we were working with Ken to create a leadership assessment. Our conversation progressed while the software loaded, and I privately wondered how a guy who fixes computer networks for a living had developed such an intense interest in leadership. He had read more than Ken Blanchard; he had read every single business book I mentioned over the course of the hour. I must have done a poor job of hiding my curiosity, because it wasn't long before he told me his story.

Richard had moved to town nine years earlier with nothing but a careful business plan, a beat-up 1978 Dodge pickup, and a knowledge of computer networks. At that time, you couldn't even find computer networking listed as a service in the phone book. He eventually grew a business from meetings in his apartment in one of the worst neighborhoods in the city to a nationwide enterprise that collected more than a million dollars a week in consulting fees. He won the Ernst & Young Entrepreneur of the Year award, was featured in *The New York Times, USA Today,* and *Maxim,* and was interviewed on television by Fox and ABC News. I blurted out the obvious question: "Then why are you here working on my computer?" The short answer was "Discipline." The long answer was that he had sold his stake in the company and was now just two months into doing it all over again. He had just nine employees in the new enterprise, and all of his technicians were committed to other jobs. He was filling in to earn our business.

Richard had not always been the model of discipline he used to make his company great. After barely graduating from high school, he threw his belongings into a backpack and pedaled his bicycle 102 miles to join his girlfriend at the University of North Carolina. Once there, he didn't have much to do while she was in class, so he spent his days in the library. Business books captured the bulk of his attention, and he read about the names etched on the archway outside the library. These were entrepreneurs who had made it big. To get your name in the archway, you had to win the Ernst & Young Entrepreneur of the Year award. He was struck most by their commitment to discipline and planning. He admired their achievements and vowed that one day his name would be etched in the archway outside the library. The books touted the merits of perseverance and planning. He wanted to develop those skills and be successful, so each day he worked diligently on a business plan.

A year later he had finalized his plan and moved out to San Diego to get started. The only apartment he could afford in the city came complete with a security system—he wedged his truck against his front door each night to keep himself in and the unsavory elements of his neighborhood out. He dedicated himself to building his business installing computer networks, and he found out quickly that keeping things on track required every ounce of devotion he could muster. He couldn't even take a day off. A missed day meant missed customers. His dependability quickly earned him the favor of local businesses seeking reliable networks.

Sticking to his business plan was not as simple as it had looked on paper. There were frequently obstacles in his path, each of which required new levels of preparation and focus. Each time the business reached a new milestone, challenges surfaced that tested his resolve. Though at times he felt he was on the verge of cracking, he never did. Today he reflects on how he taught himself discipline: "It was really hard for me in the beginning. There were a lot of little things that I had no idea you needed to do to run a business. But as I stayed focused, I found it got easier and easier to keep on track. I guess I trained my brain." As time passed, the discipline he developed turned from something new into something natural. It led him to my office the day I met him, and it helped him get his name etched among the greats in the archway.

In 1991, a couple years before Richard hopped onto his bike and pedaled to the University of North Carolina, a study was published in *Science* that threw everything neurologists knew about the brain on end.[1] The amazing revelation? That your brain is plastic. This might not seem like the most appealing term for your brain, until you consider a plastic fork. When you press one against a table, it bends easily in response to the pressure. Under the same amount of pressure, however, a metal fork remains rigid and unresponsive. Like the plastic fork, the cells in your brain have the flexibility to adjust to influences from the outside world. They do not bend back and forth as a fork does, but they grow new ways to communicate with one another in response to changing circumstances.

"Plasticity" is the term neurologists now use to describe the brain's ability to adjust to pressure and change. As Richard tolerated the discomfort that came with sticking to his long-term plan, he literally changed his brain. The more he continued on his path and surmounted new challenges, the more his brain formed connections that reinforced these acts of discipline. He wasn't aware of the mechanism behind this change, but over time he felt things getting easier. Each time he forced himself out of his comfort zone, he had less trouble the next time he faced a similar challenge.

For decades the world held the mistaken belief that the adult brain is "frozen" and unable to change. The study published in *Science* debunked this myth by revealing that learning leaves a physical mark on the brain at any age. Fresh connections in your brain make it more comfortable to use new behaviors. Your brain grows new connections much as your biceps might swell if you started curling heavy weights several times a week. The change is gradual, and the weight becomes easier and easier to lift the longer you stick to your routine. Your brain can't swell like your biceps since it's confined by your skull, so instead the brain cells develop new connections to speed the efficiency of thought without increasing its size. Each of your brain's 100 billion cells communicates by branching off small "arms" (much like a tree branch) to reach out to other cells. A single cell can grow 15,000 connections with its neighbors. As you develop new skills, the cells in the affected area branch out in a chain reaction of growth. The pathway of thought responsible for the behavior grows strong, making it easier to kick this new resource into action in the future.

As we pointed out in chapter 1, your emotional

intelligence is a product of the amount of communication between the rational and emotional centers of your brain. When you practice your emotional intelligence skills, you strengthen this pathway. Your cells literally branch out and grow connections between your feelings and your reason—but it takes time. This means that if you typically yell when you are feeling angry, for example, you have to learn to choose an alternative reaction. You must practice this new reaction many times before it will replace the urge to yell. In the beginning, doing something other than yelling when you are angry will be extremely difficult. But each time you succeed, the new pathway is strengthened. Eventually the urge to yell is so small that it's easy to ignore. To build your emotional intelligence skills, make sure the road between the rational and emotional centers of your brain is a well-traveled one.

Learning That Lasts

HOW CAN I MOVE FROM MOTIVATION TO A LASTING CHANGE?

◆

We are what we repeatedly do. Excellence, then, is not an act, but a habit.

ARISTOTLE

A chief criticism of motivational seminars is their ability to motivate. The speaker energizes and entertains the audience. They decide to make a major life change and feel that things are going to be different from now on. But the return to business as usual lacks follow-through. Nothing changes. What happened? Was it all just a bunch of hype? How can you make a lasting change?

Imagine, if you will, that you are watching a television special about children who are horribly sick. They need blood to get better, but there aren't enough donors who have their extremely rare AB negative blood type. Tears well up in your eyes as the program closes. You turn off your television and vow to donate blood once a month because you have the AB negative blood type. That very week you find the time to get to the blood bank on your lunch hour. But you find the time to do it only once more that year. Eventually you quit struggling to fit it into your hectic schedule, and you stop thinking about it altogether. Why does this happen? Are you just a bad person, too weak to remember those poor, sick children?

Every time you are enticed into adopting a new behavior, you do so because you are motivated by the effects of emotion. You turned off the television that night deeply saddened by the plight of the sick children and motivated to help them. But your emotional state was transient. It faded with time, as it was directly tied to the strong emotions generated by the program. Months later, when you tried to squeeze in a trip to the blood bank, you did not have the same level of emotion that originally drove the behavior. Because your motivation was induced by a brief and dramatic experience, you can't count on it to create a lasting change. In order for a new behavior to last, you have to practice it enough to make it permanent. You have to train your brain to adopt the behavior, and that comes only with practice. If you were to tape the television special with the sick children and watch it once a month, your chances of getting to the blood bank would increase. And if you could just make it to the blood bank a few months in a row, it's likely that your brain would adjust and new neural pathways would form to support the behavior. Suddenly, saving sick children would become a habit.

Train Your Brain

Each year on New Year's Day, more than 200 million Americans attempt to change their behavior in some way.[2] The calendar change is a perfect time to wipe the slate clean, and it motivates people to begin the process of making a change. But most people never move beyond the exciting rush of the year's first few weeks. By February 1, more than 130 million New Year's resolutions fail, as the emotional state that produced them subsides. A third of people who make resolutions keep them all year by diligently moving through the critical first six months of practice. If you practice a behavior long enough, it takes hold and perpetuates itself. It can require a tremendous effort to get a new behavior going, but once you train your brain it becomes a habit. Studies have demonstrated a lasting change in emotional intelligence more than six years after new skills were first adopted.[3] Routine behaviors last because you no longer have to think about them; you enjoy them years later because they have become a natural part of your repertoire.

As you learn new strategies for improving your emotional intelligence in the subsequent chapters of this book, remember that practice makes perfect. You won't increase your emotional intelligence simply by deciding to do things differently. You'll have to practice new behaviors repeatedly before they'll become your own. This process will strengthen the pathway between your emotions and your reason. If you practice long enough, you'll train your brain to adopt these behaviors as successful habits. Repetition of new, more emotionally intelligent behaviors will move you out of the phase of temporary motivation and into a lasting skill you can call your own.

Chapter 6

BUILDING YOUR SKILLS

PERSONAL COMPETENCE

IMPROVING HOW YOU UNDERSTAND AND MANAGE YOURSELF

◆

You don't drown by falling in the water;
you drown by staying there.

EDWIN LOUIS-COLE

Ray Charles, soul singer, songwriter, composer, and musician, learned to lean into extreme discomfort. It was the secret of his personal competence and professional success. He was a rare talent who crossed over musical styles, and his work is immortalized in the Rock and Roll Hall of Fame, the Jazz Hall of Fame, and the Blues Foundation Hall of Fame. All this from a guy whose childhood could have destroyed him.[1]

Living in poverty with his mother and younger brother during the height of the Depression, Ray didn't have much in the world. When he was five years old, his younger brother drowned in an oversized washtub. Later that same year, he began to lose his ability to see. In two short years, he was completely blind. Seven years later, while he was away at a state-run school for the blind, his mother died in her sleep at the age of thirty-two. He described his mother's death in his autobiography as "the most devastating thing in my whole experience—bar nothing, period. From that moment on, I was completely in another world. I couldn't eat. I couldn't sleep—I was totally out of it. The big problem was I couldn't cry; I couldn't get the sorrow out of my system and that made things worse."[2]

An elderly woman in town, Ma Beck, knew Ray's family well and saw how withdrawn he became after his mother's death. She literally took him aside one day and told him that his mother would have wanted him to carry on with his life and use his talent. When he described this event later as an adult, he told about crying for the first time in her arms, "howling like a tiny infant, crying for all the pain that had been stored up, crying for the loss and the grief and the sweet memories that Mama had given me." That day he leaned into his extreme pain, and eventually he used it in his music. He said that those events "were, strangely enough, extraordinarily positive for me. What I've accomplished since then, really, grows out of my coming to terms with those events."[3] Howling screams became one of his trademark contributions to popular music.

Personal competence is knowing yourself and doing the most you can with what you have. It's not about being perfect or having complete control of your emotions. Rather, it's about allowing your feelings to inform you and to guide your behavior. Ray's emotions helped him make powerful music. He didn't develop personal competence easily; it took years. In the process he overcame drug addiction and embattled relationships. Over time, Ray fully realized the ability to let his sorrow join the music welling up inside him. He enjoyed an amazing life and career, guided by all of his emotions.

Lean into the Discomfort

As shown by our own research, the biggest obstacle to increased personal competence is the tendency to avoid the discomfort that comes from increasing your self-awareness. More than two thirds of the people we have tested have great difficulty admitting their short-comings. Things you do not think about are off your radar for a reason: they can sting when they surface. Avoiding this pain creates problems, because it is a short-term fix. Leaning into your discomfort is the only way to change. You cannot manage yourself adequately if you ignore what you need to do to change.

Rather than avoiding a feeling, your goal should be to move toward it, into it, and eventually through it. This can be said for even mild emotional discomfort, such as boredom, confusion, or anticipation. When you ignore or minimize an emotion, no matter how small or insignificant, you miss the opportunity to do something productive with it. Even worse, ignoring your feelings does not make them go away; it just helps them to surface again when you least expect it. Business thought leader Peter Drucker says that to better manage oneself, each of us needs to discover our own arrogance.[4] We all have things we dismiss as being too unimportant for us to bother learning more about. In the realm of personal competence, one person thinks that apologies are for sissies, so she never learns to recognize when one is called for. Another person hates feeling down, so he spends all his time being the life of the party. Both of these people need to take the bold step of moving into the feelings that will enable a change. Otherwise, they will continue down an unproductive, unsatisfying path, repeating the same patterns over and over again.

After the first few times you allow yourself to focus on discomfort, you will quickly find that the discomfort isn't so bad, it doesn't ruin you, and it reaps rewards. For instance, the medical student in college who is shy should start practicing early on how to overcome his aversion to saying "Hi" to those around him, because developing a rapport with his patients will be essential to his success. He will have to be the one to say hello first. To learn to do so, he has to become aware of his aversion and the importance of overcoming it. The surprising thing about increasing your self-awareness is that just thinking about it will help you change, even though much of your focus will initially be on the things you do "wrong." Don't be afraid of your emotional "mistakes." They tell you what you should be doing differently and provide the steady stream of information you need to understand yourself as life unfolds.

To improve your ability to recognize emotions, consider the range of emotions people express. We have so many words to describe the feelings that surface in life, yet all emotions are derivations of five core feelings: happiness, sadness, anger, fear, and shame. The complexity of these emotions is revealed when you look at how they are expressed in varying forms of intensity. Look at the range of emotions in the table on the following page. Can you think of examples from your own life that demonstrate each degree of intensity for the five core emotions? To become more personally competent, identify which emotions in this table you tend to feel more often than others. This will raise your emotional self-awareness and provide a guide as to how you might manage these emotions when they surface.

Feeling a range of emotions is not the same as self-awareness. To accurately recognize an emotion, you also have to pay attention to your internal thermostat—the thoughts and physical signs that accompany a feeling. These signs are not the feelings themselves but the beliefs and sensations that accompany them. High self-awareness is recognizing the sensations that you feel and being able to name which emotion is happening. Everyone's thermostat reads differently. Thoughts and physical sensations are your perfectly normal responses to emotionally arousing situations. Your thoughts might speed up or your mind go blank. You might feel hot, cold, or numb. Your heart might skip a beat or race. You might feel muscle tension or see with tunnel vision.

Intensity of Feelings	HAPPY	SAD	ANGRY	AFRAID	ASHAMED
High	Elated Excited Overjoyed Thrilled Exuberant Ecstatic Fired up Delighted	Depressed Disappointed Alone Hurt Dejected Hopeless Sorrowful Miserable	Furious Enraged Outraged Aggravated Irate Seething	Terrified Horrified Scared stiff Petrified Fearful Panicky	Sorrowful Remorseful Unworthy Worthless Disgraced Dishonored
Medium	Cheerful Up Good Relieved Satisfied	Heartbroken Down Upset Distressed Regretful Melancholy	Upset Mad Hot Frustrated Agitated Disgusted	Scared Frightened Threatened Insecure Uneasy Shocked	Apologetic Defamed Sneaky Guilty
Mild	Glad Contented Pleasant Fine Pleased	Unhappy Moody Blue Lost Bad Dissatisfied	Perturbed Annoyed Uptight Put out Irritated Touchy	Apprehensive Nervous Worried Timid Unsure Anxious	Embarrassed Disappointed Let down

The five core emotions run left to right across the top of the table. Manifestations of each emotion based upon the intensity felt are described down each of the columns in the table.[5]

Your throat might feel tight, or you might notice tingling in a limb. An executive we know gives a great description of the physical signs that accompany his anger: "When someone tells me a decision I made is dumb, my sensations are always the same. I feel my chest get hot and turn red. Since I wear a shirt and tie all day, no one but me can tell when it happens."

The same is true with your tendencies; how you usually respond to various situations and people is unique to you. One of the universally uncomfortable feelings people have as they work on personal competence is the feeling of being unfinished, of not yet mastering it. We fear making a mistake in front of others who might see us practicing. Personal development requires making many mistakes even though it is uncomfortable to recognize when we make them. We catch ourselves getting carried away, or maybe we catch ourselves trying to repress our emotions and turn them off. These are the moments when we need to try something different. Working on emotional intelligence skills requires that we take responsibility for our part of the difficulties we face.

Practicing emotional intelligence skills is how we become sophisticated in our ability to spot and use emotions to our advantage in every situation possible. The people we know who are "extremely emotionally intelligent" are simply the people who got a head start in this process. They may have started at an early age, as Ray Charles did, when life experiences threw them challenges to deal with. They likely made mistakes along the way and found their challenges as tough as those you currently face. Rest assured: they too have many stories of failed early attempts to develop emotional intelligence. Now they appear to be cruising and their skills appear easily acquired, even magically maintained. Don't be fooled.

People high in emotional intelligence have been leaning into their discomfort, making mistakes, practicing, and getting better at their skills for years. If you are one of these people, we encourage you to think about where you can focus your efforts on a situation that is particularly important to you right now. We all have something that we are ignoring. If you are like the rest of us—new to the idea of emotional intelligence, yet filled with life experience—you will benefit from leaning into the discomfort of your emotions by using the following techniques.

Manage Your Tendencies

Recently we talked with a room of people about their life experiences with each of the emotional intelligence skills. We asked them what works best in managing their behavior. Three men from the group sang the praises of becoming more comfortable with telling people what they don't like to do. Specifically, they meant speaking up at work and admitting that they didn't like being involved in certain kinds of projects and weren't even very good at them. For them, self-management was overcoming the discomfort of admitting a "flaw." It meant being assertive instead of sitting quietly and agreeing to do whatever was asked of them. All three men were in their late forties and early fifties, and it had taken the bulk of their careers for them to take this action. Before they could make a move, they had to learn their tendencies and then overcome the fear of being perceived as uncooperative.

Self-management is more than resisting an explosive or problematic behavior. Perhaps the biggest challenge that people face is managing their tendencies over time and applying their skills in a variety of situations. Obvious and momentary opportunities for self-control (e.g., "I'm so mad at that darn dog!") are the easiest to spot and manage. Real results come from putting your momentary needs on hold to pursue larger, more important goals.[6] The realization of such goals is often delayed, meaning that your commitment to self-management will be tested over and over again. Those who manage themselves the best are able to see things through without cracking. Success comes to those who can put their needs on hold and continually manage their tendencies.

Building Your Skills

If you are just beginning to recognize your patterns of emotion and discomfort, write down some of the things that you see, do, think, and feel in situations that are upsetting or overwhelming for you. This will help you to discover what behaviors you fall victim to when your emotions get the best of you. Talk to friends and colleagues to gain further insight. They can help you recognize your patterns and make the connection between something that happens and the way you respond. This description may just be the missing link you need.

Leaning into the discomfort of self-management also includes planning for the discomfort ahead of time. If you anticipate having a difficult conversation with the director of the PTA at your child's school, take a few minutes to plan how you are going to handle your frustration. Decide what you will and will not say. If every time you walk into the local electronic warehouse you get excited about the new gadgets there and leave with something you didn't really need or can't afford, plan your strategy for dealing with the disappointment of leaving empty-handed. Your tendencies when faced with strong emotion are an important part of who you are. Just as preparation for a marathon leads to better performance, preparation for a difficult situation improves your ability to manage yourself in the moment.

When you can't plan ahead because the discomfort of an emotion surprises you, pause before doing anything in response to it. You might need a few seconds, a day, or weeks. If you need just a few moments, take a deep breath. When emotions run strong, it is best to slow down and think a bit before moving forward. If your teenage son pushes you with that one phrase that makes you feel something close to rage, the best thing to do is to take a deep breath, say you can't talk right now, and leave the room to find space to think and calm down. It may require leaving the house for a while before you return and respond.

Managing your tendencies requires you to have some perspective on an emotion-arousing situation and then acting on it. If you are cut off while approaching an intersection, you might feel an impulse to tailgate the car in front of you to show your disapproval of the other person's inept driving and "thank" him or her for putting you in danger. But if you stop to think for a moment, you will realize that tailgating is going to put you in more danger than you are in now. If the other driver slams on the brakes, you will have less time to stop. Violent road rage on the part of the other driver also isn't out of the question. Your emotions are frustration and anger, but you can recognize these feelings. You can reflect and realize that continuing the game of chicken will only prolong them. You can choose to drive on without even looking at the other driver. A couple of minutes later, you are calm again. Your momentary need was revenge, but you have self-managed your counterproductive impulse and can go on with your day. This is personal competence in action.

Talking to yourself may seem an odd piece of advice, but self-talk is a powerful method for taking control of your next move, even your next emotion.[7] We do not mean talking to yourself out loud but privately, inside your head. We all do it, and, whether we know it or not, what we say to ourselves has a tremendous impact on our behavior. If you want to call a girl you know and ask her for a date, you may never do it if the message running inside your head keeps saying "She is going to say no. Why would she ever want to go out with me?" Self-talk changes the script inside your head to something more enabling, such as, "What have I got to lose? I'm never gonna know if I don't call. Who knows? Maybe she'll say yes." The amazing thing about self-talk, because it can sound so childish, is that it's one of the most powerful determinants of what we do. Ray Charles told himself that he had to keep going because his mother would have wanted him to. This is a much more empowering message to have running through your head than "Why should I bother, my whole family is gone. No one even cares what happens to me."

Talking to others is also a great way to understand and manage your tendencies. Ask for advice from someone who may see your behavior a little more objectively. If the situation is extremely difficult or complex, you may want to get third and fourth opinions. There is nothing worse than being bogged down by a single opinion that is just as skewed as your own. The point is not necessarily to ask other people what you should do but to ask them how they see the situation. Do they see you as being led by your emotions? Do you come across differently than you expect? Other people can give you all the information you need to manage your tendencies and take yourself in the direction you want to go. For Ray Charles, an uninvited second opinion changed his life.

Social Competence

LISTENING SO PEOPLE WILL TALK AND TALKING SO PEOPLE WILL LISTEN

◆

When dealing with people, remember that you are not dealing with creatures of logic but creatures of emotion.

DALE CARNEGIE

Rebecca worked for a large retail chain in the Midwest. She loved her job, but her boss constantly pushed her buttons and made the work unbearable. Finally she approached the vice president of human resources and described her situation. She detailed her boss's two most frustrating habits: cutting her off in the middle of a sentence and always being too busy to meet with her. Rebecca's boss was so unaware of these behaviors that he didn't know that she and other members of his staff were on the brink of leaving the company. The human resources VP decided to take action. Rebecca was a valuable employee, and the company didn't want to lose her.

Rebecca's situation was easier to solve than you might imagine. The VP of human resources was already coaching other managers and decided to meet with Rebecca's boss to give him feedback on his emotional intelligence skills. First, she initiated a 360-degree survey to gather feedback from his staff. Each member of his staff had the opportunity to anonymously answer questions online about the boss's skill in dealing with people and managing his behavior. When he reviewed his emotional intelligence scores during the coaching session, he was shocked by the feedback. He had no clue that his social skills were a problem for those who worked for him. Like many people who are extremely low in social competence, he wasn't aware of how people reacted to him. He and the VP of human resources worked through a plan whereby he would take two simple actions to improve this skill: he would pause and listen when his employees spoke to him, and he would carve out time to meet regularly with his staff, without interruptions. Though he was a bit robotic about it at first, the skills were simple enough to adopt.

For Rebecca, these two simple changes made all the difference. He didn't become the perfect boss, but she appreciated his effort and felt more comfortable working for him. He took the time to meet with her regularly, and she could tell he was listening when she spoke to him. She was relieved that he could master these two activities. In a little over a month they turned the situation around, and Rebecca decided to stay with the company.

How to Listen So People Will Talk

Listening is the most important thing you can do to build social awareness. It's also really hard work and requires a unique blend of self-management and multitasking. To listen well, we have to stop doing many things we like to do. We have to stop talking, stop the monologue that may be running through our mind, stop anticipating the point the other person is about to make, and stop thinking ahead to what we are going to say next. At home this will likely involve something simple, such as muting the television or setting down your book and turning to the family member who is talking to you. At work, it can be done by closing your door, turning off your cell phone, and putting down your documents to face the person who is talking. Your silence and attention are all it will take to get the other person talking. When you remove all the discouraging barriers from conversation, people feel respected and heard.

People take in information from their world through the five senses: taste, touch, smell, sight, and sound. Most of us take in the majority of information about our interactions with others through just two of the senses, hearing and seeing. This offers us just two sources of information to assess what is really going on. Your sixth sense is your perception of emotions, and it's the most important way of gathering information during an interaction with another person. Consider the last time you were talking to someone and the words made logical sense, but something subtle about the conversation made things awkward. Perhaps you felt that the other person was just going through the motions and wasn't really happy to be there talking. It probably made you feel distant or ignored; such feelings are critical to your observation of the situation. They are real pieces of information you can use to adjust your reaction and determine the best course of action.

One thing you can do to learn to listen so people will talk is become an anthropologist. Anthropologists make their living watching others in their natural state without letting their own thoughts and feelings disturb the observation. This is social awareness in its purest form. You can play the anthropologist's role anytime by keeping surveillance on your mind. The surveillance approach is a simple way to distract your mind from your own thoughts and feelings. It will help you focus on what is happening around you, and people will respond well to your attention. You'll also understand more about what people are saying and doing, as well as why they act the way they do. You'll be surprised by what you notice about others when your thoughts are more on them than on yourself.

It takes practice to identify what another person is feeling and understand how those feelings are influencing his or her behavior. This is the challenge in developing the social awareness skills of social competence. Professional poker players spend inordinate amounts of time learning to read the subtlest of cues coming from one another. You don't have to go this far, because people are visibly influenced by their emotions all the time. To develop your social awareness skills, all you have to do is pay attention to their body language, tone and volume of voice, and speed of movement. These will give you the information you need to determine how they are feeling. Be sure to ask questions when you aren't sure what's going on with the other person. It's an easy way to improve the accuracy of your perception, and it makes people feel good to know you are paying attention. A simple clarifying question, such as, "Does this mean you're disappointed?" is an incredible tool and will help you avoid misinterpreting the other person's experience.

How to Talk So People Will Listen

The weaker a connection you have with someone, the harder it is to get your point across. If you want people to listen, you have to practice relationship management and seek benefits from every relationship, especially the challenging ones. The difference between an interaction and a relationship is a matter of frequency. It's a product of the quality, depth, and time you spend interacting with another person. When you first meet someone, your time together may be brief, and the quality and depth will be relatively superficial. As you build a history with this person, a relationship will start to form. Whether it becomes a surface relationship, a genuine friendship, or anything in between will depend upon your ability to manage interactions. Now we'll focus on your part in the equation.

First, discover what role emotions play in your interactions with others. Emotions play a part in every discussion between people, no matter how light. Whether your mood is good or bad, excited or bored, think about how it affects the back-and-forth between you and the other person. If you notice when your feelings are taking over, you will be much less confused by the interaction. If the other person is someone who can join you in leaning into the discomfort, you can talk about it together to prevent problems in the future.

There will always be times where bringing up emotions is a mistake (bad timing or just not the other person's cup of tea), but you can usually recognize these situations by using your social awareness skills. If you can take a moment to stop and talk about "what is really going on," it will diffuse the power of the feelings. There's no need to play "shrink" with the other person; just mention what you are seeing and ask if there is another way the two of you can tackle the problem in light of this information. Be careful not to point a finger or avoid your part in the problem. The goal is to find a balance among what you hear being said, how it is being said, and the feelings that are emanating from both parties.

To find out how emotions are involved in every interaction between two people, tune in to even the most benign events. Conversations about weekend errands, discussions of family gatherings, debates over current events, and negotiations sometimes stall for no apparent reason. Things usually fall apart when personal attachments ("We spent the holiday with your family last year!") get in the way of resolution. The parties involved will continue to disagree until the emotional involvement is addressed. When it is the other person who is being emotional, attend to what he or she is feeling without being threatening. In addressing the other person's feelings, you must try to be supportive, whether or not you agree with his or her actions. Being too direct in addressing the other person's feelings will usually lead to defensiveness. When you are the one who is becoming emotional, try your best to take responsibility for your half of the problem. If you need more time to understand your emotions or even to calm down, ask for it politely and assertively. Things will likely go more smoothly when you can accurately explain what you are feeling.

There is no middle ground for emotions. When they happen, they have either a positive or negative impact on every interaction between two people. Therefore, it is always important to show when you care. If you have a genuine interest in someone, do not hide it, even if there are only certain things you like about him or her. People like people who like them, and they enjoy positive feedback. People will always remember a compliment that is well thought out, accurate, and sincere. Whenever you show you care, you help other people to better understand what is important to you. The extra time you take to offer help, support, encouragement, or interest will be time well spent. It will go a long way in building a relationship.

FOUR

Going Places

Chapter 7

BRINGING EMOTIONAL INTELLIGENCE TO WORK

TAKING YOUR GAME TO THE NEXT LEVEL

HOW CAN YOU USE EMOTIONAL INTELLIGENCE TO ADVANCE YOUR CAREER?

◆

Don't bother just to be better than your contemporaries or predecessors. Try to be better than yourself.

WILLIAM FAULKNER

Emotions don't stay home just because we head to work. They stick with us all day like an annoying bunch of backseat drivers. The sooner you become aware of your emotions and get to know them well, the sooner you will take back control of your work. Understanding and managing your emotions is the only way to get the most from each day and head where you want to go in your career. Although in our own work emotional challenges surface daily, one evening we shared stands out as a poignant example. It illustrates emotions we understood and managed to our benefit, as well as others that took us by surprise.

That evening, we arrived at the north tower of a high-rise hotel in downtown San Diego to kick off an emotional intelligence certification program. Many professional trainers were in attendance, looking to build their repertoire of programs. There's always pressure when we speak to these groups. Participants come from all over the United States and other parts of the world, and they expect a lot from the training. The seminar room was located on the mezzanine floor, a comfortable distance from the hustle and bustle of the city streets below. The seminar team was well prepared, and things kicked off to a smooth start. Little did we know that a visitor was sneaking into the hotel through the service door.

Travis was standing by the podium explaining

the finer points of social competence when a stranger entered. He was easily six feet tall, with dark, matted hair, drooping shoulders, and heavily stained clothes. You could hear a pin drop as he made his way between the maze of tables crowding the floor. His filthy clothes brushed several of the attendees as he made his way to the front of the room. The stranger stopped directly in front of Travis and took a seat. Even though he was no longer standing, his presence was larger than life.

As a trained speaker is bound to do, Travis didn't show the audience how much of a surprise this was. Unexpected situations arise far too often when you're in front of an audience, and letting them know you're losing control is a death march. After a brief moment, the visitor leaned forward to Travis and asked softly, "Can I have a glass of water?" Travis looked over at the man and then to the sweaty pitcher of ice water in front of him and the six empty glasses circling it. Hard to say no to that, he thought. He smiled at the audience and poured his guest a glass of water. After taking a drink the man leaned back in his chair, crossed his legs, and settled in for a thought-provoking evening on emotional intelligence.

Travis continued on with his presentation, keeping a wary eye on the scruffy new stranger in the front row. Jean was waiting to speak, standing on the side of the room closest to the doors. Her mind churned through many thoughts at once: Clearly a homeless man. But why is he being so bold? He was so intentional about going to the front of the room. Is he going to start harassing our participants? How did he get in here in the first place? She looked at Travis, who was gallantly moving forward, though no one in the room—herself included—could concentrate on a word he was saying. She snapped back into the realization that she would have to be the one to do something. She took Travis's calmness as a silent "Okay, Jean, I'll stall them while you go get the hotel staff." She bolted out the door.

Her dash down the seemingly infinitely long corridor was complicated by her new black skirt and heels. Jean's thoughts raced with her: Why isn't there anyone in the other conference rooms? How are Travis and the audience doing back there? Where are the hotel staff? Arrrgggh! She found her first hotel staff person in the business center and quickly explained the situation. The woman behind the counter immediately picked up the phone to dial Security. The voice on the other end assured her that help would arrive shortly.

Her confidence bolstered a little, Jean ran back to the room. When she entered, she found Travis right where she had left him, speaking in front of a large room of very quiet people. She could sense what a strange experience this was for the audience.

She peeked out the door down the long hallway: not a security guard in sight. She fidgeted in the doorway while a couple more minutes passed. Finally she'd had enough. Her heart still racing from the run, Jean held up her hands and yelled over Travis's voice echoing from the speakers, "Why don't we all take a break out in the hallway?" People sprang from their chairs like students hearing the bell signaling the start of summer. Just as the last audience members exited the room, security guards in rubber gloves burst through the door and made a beeline for the homeless man, still seated in the front row.

The unexpected visitor that evening demonstrated just how loud emotions can get and how easily they can drown out the work at hand. Our hushed seminar room was screaming with intense feelings. Did they get in the way of the task at hand? Absolutely. It's unlikely that anyone will remember what Travis presented while the stranger was in the room that night. Everyone will certainly remember the visitor and how he or she felt while he was there. He even made it into this book! That is the power of emotions at work.

Defining Moments

We work hard to understand emotional intelligence and make it accessible to people everywhere. We work closely together and often find we have unique emotions and perspectives on the same situation. As Jean stood at the side of the seminar room, her thoughts put her on immediate alert. Travis's experience working with the mentally ill gave him a different perspective: he recognized the man as a likely sufferer of the "negative" form of schizophrenia. People in this state typically lack the energy or motivation to harm others. Travis was also motivated to maintain his train of thought and avoid looking out of control. He continued speaking in the hope that the situation would be resolved quickly.

The tension in the room that evening dragged on too long. Travis's emotional experience of the situation was not in line with that of the audience members. One woman, whose husband works with the homeless, praised Travis for how he had dealt with the man. But the majority of the audience felt nervous. Both women and men were uncomfortable with the visitor and wanted the session to break up immediately. This all happened shortly after the tragedy of September 11, 2001, and multiple audience members feared that the man's layers of clothing might hide a bomb or other dangerous weapon.

How did so much happen in just a few moments? Everyone we spoke to later told us that the situation had aroused strong emotions. Some said that the moment the man walked in the room, you could feel the tension in the air. Travis used self-management to stay poised in front of the audience, but ironically—he was speaking about social awareness—he didn't focus enough on the others' feelings to make them comfortable. A closer look at the audience members' faces would have cued him to stop speaking. He fell into a common trap of a social situation that arouses strong emotion: having to stay more focused on others than on yourself to maneuver through it successfully. Jean also fell into a common emotional trap. Her emotions had her running down the hall looking for Security, when a little more reflection should have sent her back to the room to break the session first. Once she was back in the room and paused for a moment to think, she quickly realized she could cut through the tension by calling for a break. It's even interesting that no one in the audience raised a hand to request a break, even though all of them had studied group training methods. Emotions were driving everyone's actions—or inactions—that night.

All the emotions we felt that evening served a purpose. They motivated us to think and take action. The better we understood our emotions, the easier it was to move through the problem. The balance between thought and feeling defined our level of success, as it always will in difficult situations. There was no clear right or wrong way to address the challenge before us. This is usually the case. Only when we reviewed the situation later did we discover that some of our actions had been more effective than others. The renowned Harvard Business School professor Joseph L. Badaracco, Jr., describes how the moments that shape our careers are often those when we must choose between right and right.[1] When there is no right or wrong answer, emotions are critical. They are usually the deciding factor that enables us to choose one direction or the other. If you use your emotional intelligence skills at work, they will steer you through the important decisions that will define your career.

Most days at work do not include homeless people joining you unannounced, but emotions are often as active, varied, and ready to surface as they were for us that evening. Understand that emotions will at times appear to take over, but you always retain the option of managing them to achieve some purpose. Taking emotional intelligence to work means becoming more adept at noticing the emotions you feel in a variety of situations, getting better at managing the feelings that get in your way, and giving yourself permission to practice new behaviors. You bring your feelings to work each day, whether you pay attention to them or not. Emotions are present in every conversation you have, every phone call you take, and every decision you make.

The intensity and variety of emotions that can

surface over the course of a day are astounding. We find that people experience an average of 27 emotions each waking hour. With nearly 17 waking hours each day, you have about 456 emotional experiences from the time you get up until the time you go to bed. This means that more than 3,000 emotional reactions guide you through each week and more than 150,000 each year! Of all the emotions you will experience in your lifetime, nearly two million of them will happen during working hours. It's no wonder that people who manage emotions well are easier to work with and more likely to achieve what they set out to do.

Communication and Quiet Conflict

Communication and conflict are paired because they are practically mutually exclusive. It is hard to have one of them if you have the other. But strangely, good communication can't always prevent large conflicts in the workplace. Why? Because you can't completely avoid conflict. The key is to work through issues and important problems before they grow to the point that they are considered to be conflicts. Conflict results from avoiding an issue and failing to address it constructively head-on. Interpersonal conflicts, like all our problems, need to be addressed when they are big enough to see, yet still small enough to solve.

Quiet conflict grows with unspoken signals, backhanded comments, and bubbling tension. Quiet conflict feeds off of a lack of communication and a lack of effort to understand why the other person is defensive or seething. Quiet conflict is the result of issues that fester long enough to let emotional involvement grow beyond the point of acting rationally. Damaged pride and hurt feelings are the first signs of quiet conflict. They signal that the parties involved have moved beyond the point of being constructive. How does simple poor communication grow into quiet conflict? Let's examine a typical situation at work to see how it can grow into a conflict:

> You are in your office working on an important document. Lynne walks in with an idea for the project the two of you are currently tasked with. Less than a minute into her commentary, something she says reminds you that you forgot to return an important call from a customer you met last week. You suddenly feel anxious, and from then on nothing Lynne says matters. You want this feeling to go away, but it won't until you make the call.

A common response we see in this situation involves letting Lynne continue talking, completely unaware that you have tuned her out. As you dwell on the problem and try to figure out how you are going to handle it, she moves through her points, assuming that the odd look on your face is a sign of disapproval. Finally she finishes and you rush her out of your office, telling her that you have something important to take care of. To spare yourself the embarrassment of the situation you have created with the customer, you skirt the details of why you are sending Lynne out the door so quickly. This is likely to leave Lynne thinking that you don't care to listen to any opinions other than your own. Without an explanation on your part, all she sees is the odd look on your face and your cold distance from the discussion. Such a response leaves room for improvement because your feelings about the forgotten call taint the current interaction. Now you have two problems: the late call and a resentful coworker.

What would the emotionally intelligent response in this situation be? It would probably be to let the realization of the forgotten call sink in for a moment and pause to catch your breath. Without wasting any more time, you should speak up and tell Lynne what you need to go do and how it's affecting your state of mind. You should ask for her understanding and quickly schedule time to loop back with her later that day. Lynne would leave your office so you could make the call, and later that morning you could drop by her office to show that you want to continue the conversation. This response is emotionally intelligent because it leads you to productive action while taking care of your current responsibility to your coworker. Lynne will likely notice this and appreciate it. In the heat of the moment, it's unlikely that most people will successfully address all of the concerns above. Worry about a customer is certain to cloud anyone's thinking. Good communication comes from having the courage to tell Lynne what's going on right away—no matter how you do it. When you explain yourself to Lynne, you create an opportunity to connect with her and keep two troublesome situations from simmering the rest of the day.

Bringing Emotional Intelligence to Work

Taking Your Team to the Next Level

HOW CAN YOUR TEAM USE EMOTIONAL INTELLIGENCE TO ACHIEVE ITS GOALS?

◆

Whatever we have accomplished has been because other people have helped us.

WALT DISNEY

Experts agreed that the space shuttle *Challenger* would explode if it were launched in very cold weather. It was 36° Fahrenheit when *Challenger* took off on January 28, 1986, and several engineers had made attempts to cancel the flight. Why did NASA launch anyway? While official documents put the blame on two causes—malfunction of a special part called an O-ring and gross mismanagement by both NASA executives and their contractors—a lack of team emotional intelligence also contributed to the tragic accident.[2]

Roger Boisjoly was an experienced engineer who joined the O-ring improvement effort the summer before the launch. He worked for months attempting to fix its cold-weather defects, but in the end his team was unable to create a seal that would hold in extreme circumstances. The day before the launch, they delivered fourteen viewgraphs in a presentation to NASA executives, detailing their concerns about the risks of conducting a launch at the forecasted temperature. The only quantifiable data the group had to prove their concern was outdated. They ended their presentation with the recommendation not to launch below 53°.[3]

The NASA group at the Kennedy Space Center did not receive the news well. They deliberated briefly and came back with the news that they intended to launch. Their expert argued that launching in the cold could be a nonissue. Roger's boss turned to his team and announced that they needed to make a management decision. Roger snatched a photograph that demonstrated the risk of launching in the cold and threw it onto the table. His teammate Arnie jumped in to explain and drew a picture of the problem. Their boss stood unflinchingly, with an unfriendly look in his eyes. He was not interested in their explanation. Roger and his team sat helplessly while four executives from his company held a closed-door discussion, then returned to the meeting and recommended a launch to NASA.

Roger's team, feeling defeated, stood by angry but silent while NASA accepted the recommendation to launch. He later said, "The change in decision so upset me that I do not remember Stanley Reinhartz of NASA asking if anyone had anything else to say over the teleconference. The teleconference was then disconnected so I immediately left the room." The engineering team's feelings of helplessness smothered their fury. When asked if they had any final comments, they chose not to remind their superiors and the team from NASA of their recommendation to cancel the launch. The team's judgment foretold a disaster, yet they passively accepted their superiors' decision. They overlooked the difference between typical feelings of frustration and exceptional feelings of anger, sadness, fury, and helplessness.

The Power of Team Emotional Intelligence

Just as a person has emotional intelligence skills, a group of people working as a team have a collective emotional intelligence. As in the case of Roger's engineering team, emotions can explain how a group will act in unison. Team emotional intelligence is a group's style of relating to one another, making decisions, and responding to other groups in the organization. This concept was first introduced in 1998 in the *Harvard Business Review*.[4] Members of emotionally intelligent teams respond constructively in emotionally uncomfortable situations, influencing one another positively. Simply put, members of emotionally intelligent teams get better results and experience deeper satisfaction from working together. The basic model for team emotional intelligence is similar to that of individual emotional intelligence, though the largest part of the focus is on the team as a group.

Team emotional intelligence focuses heavily on management skills: managing the emotions of the team members, managing the relationships among the team members, and managing the relationships that the team has with outside individuals and groups. The core awareness skill is simply being able to identify and understand emotions as they surface among group members. The four core team emotional intelligence skills are emotional awareness, emotion management, internal relationship management, and external relationship management.

Team Emotional Awareness

Team emotional awareness is the team's ability to accurately perceive the emotions that influence the group. This includes recognizing how each team member tends to respond to specific situations and people. For example, consider a team whose presentation to the CEO has just been postponed a month.

EMOTIONAL AWARENESS	EMOTION MANAGEMENT
INTERNAL RELATIONSHIP MANAGEMENT	EXTERNAL RELATIONSHIP MANAGEMENT

Team emotional intelligence is made up of four skills that include awareness of the emotions that surface in the team members' work together, how they manage emotions, and how they manage relationships both inside the team and with outside parties.

They have been working hard on this project together, and the setback is badly timed. The team collectively feels this is a big disappointment, and the group members sit around the table griping about all the things that will not get done according to the deadlines they have projected. A team with emotional awareness skills will recognize the frustration and discontent in the air and allow members to express their disappointment. Stifling this type of expression will only prolong the griping. The team must discuss what its various members are feeling and how it will influence their plans. The team's awareness will only make its planning more effective.

Team emotional awareness is a large product of how well members recognize the emotions that surface and influence their work. Do people know what happens to the team when members are bored, overly excited, defensive, losing hope, or threatened? Do members have similar or different reactions to the same situations? Are feelings taking over discussions, or are they repressed and never explored? The answers to these questions indicate a team's emotional tendencies. Tendencies are repeated patterns of responding when emotions surface in the group. The team members should explore the group's tendencies with emotions in order to build their emotional awareness skills. Just as organizations have cultures in which certain behaviors are encouraged and others discouraged, each team develops its own microculture. There are unspoken rules about how much or how little emotions can be acknowledged and explored. Some teams relish strong feelings, whereas others will avoid an uncomfortable feeling at all costs. The emotionally aware team recognizes important emotional signals as key information that should be used to help get results.

Team Emotion Management

Team emotion management is the team members' ability to use their awareness of the group's emotions as a whole to be flexible and direct behavior in a positive direction. This means managing the collective emotional reaction of the team in response to a given situation. Teams that can manage these tendencies are far more productive than those that cannot.[5] Using the team whose presentation to the CEO was postponed as an example, will the group members wallow in their disappointment by stalling all progress on the project for a month? Maybe they will make the next four meetings gripe sessions—or, better yet, maybe the next four meetings will be canceled altogether. An emotionally intelligent team would manage members' emotions and use them to motivate efforts to strengthen their presentation during the extra time given. A team with effective emotion management skills will have at least one or two members who will pull the group out of the doldrums and get everyone back on track. This does not mean telling the group to get over their disappointment, but instead to feel it as well as begin looking constructively toward what is next.

Team emotion management is one of the more difficult team emotional intelligence skills because most of the members of any group are not yet comfortable managing their emotions publicly or discussing emotions in a group setting. It requires a group of people to work together to spot when emotions are steering their progress. They have to stop and ask themselves if their progress will be helped or hurt by bringing their emotions to the surface. For example, if the group is feeling excited and motivated after a visit from a top executive who has thanked them for what they've accomplished, their willingness to take risks and to be more creative will be bolstered. Similarly, if excitement turns into overzealousness or imperviousness to mistakes, the team could overlook significant risk. The important step after feeling the excitement is to couple it with reason and action. Managing emotions as a group requires noticing when emotions are playing a role and managing them so the team can move forward.

Internal Relationship Management

Internal relationship management refers to the team members' ability to interact effectively with one another in order to respond well to difficult or challenging situations. This is the sum of each team member's ability to interact constructively with all other team members. For example, suppose one team member has been experiencing a high level of stress at home lately and is having trouble producing reports on time and without errors. The team depends on these reports for making decisions. Should the team avoid confronting the situation by tolerating the reports as they are? Should the other team members pressure this person even more by sending curt e-mail reminders? Or might there be a team member who can stop by his office to offer support and help him draft the reports? Efforts at managing relationships within the group serve to strengthen the bond between team members. Team members who manage relationships with the rest of the group, both during and outside meetings, minimize the challenges that come up when emotions are strong.

A team's internal relationship management skills are strengthened by the ability of each team member to practice social competence. The team's performance is enhanced when each team member takes responsibility for being aware of his or her emotions.

During team meetings, self-management and social awareness are critical for everyone in the room to avoid problems such as interrupting or ignoring people or putting them down. Each team member is responsible for developing and maintaining a positive—or at least productive—working relationship with every other team member.

External Relationship Management

External relationship management is the team's ability to act effectively as a group across organizational boundaries. Consider a design team that invites a member of the quality assurance group to its final planning session for a new product. Do the team members treat the person as an outsider to be ignored, as a member of their extended team, or as an unwelcome guest? The team that can proactively welcome the advice and concerns of another group that has the power to make a go/no-go decision is the team that is using external relationship management skills to its benefit. These relationships often propel a team's objectives forward, and teams that pay no attention to it often lag down the path to their goals.

Very often, teams focus solely on relationships within the group, and this creates pitfalls for them in the long run. A high-performing team may celebrate a little too zealously, forgetting to thank those outside the team who helped to make their achievements possible. When difficulties face this team in the future, outside parties may not feel like going the extra mile to help out. Teams also have to compete for resources or to get their projects approved. External relationship management means that team determines who has a good relationship with the decision maker who will determine what that team needs. The team can select an ambassador to create visibility or support for its work. Work accomplished in groups is dependent upon influence. The O-ring engineering team had the critical facts prepared, yet they weren't able to influence the decision makers outside their group. The groundwork—good working relationships with those outside the team—had not been laid in advance.

Seventeen years after the *Challenger* disaster, the *Columbia* space shuttle was lost as it reentered the atmosphere. An important cause of the crash, cited by the Columbia Accident Investigation Board, was the decision making at NASA post-*Challenger* The Rogers Commission found a NASA "blinded by its 'Can-Do' attitude, a cultural artifact of the Apollo era that was inappropriate in a space shuttle program so strapped by schedule pressures and shortages that spare parts had to be cannibalized from one vehicle to launch another."[6] After the *Columbia* shuttle was launched, dangerous foam debris was identified that would jeopardize its ability to land safely. Engineering teams responded to cost and schedule demands over safety concerns. They suggested potential ways for landing the shuttle, rather than plans for a rescue mission. Swayed by the prevailing culture at NASA, they lacked the team emotional intelligence skills needed to rise above the policy and rescue the ill-fated mission.

Improving Team Emotional Intelligence

Though formal research on team emotional intelligence is still in its infancy, it has been clearly demonstrated that emotionally intelligent teams achieve their goals and contribute more to the success of organizations than those that are not. Teams that score low in an assessment of workgroup emotional intelligence underperform when compared with their counterparts with high emotional intelligence. Specifically, their ability to focus on tasks and achieve their goals is significantly lower than that of teams that score high in emotional intelligence. Training in emotional intelligence skills improves a team's job performance and emotional intelligence scores. It improves a group's ability to focus and brings its performance into line with that of teams that are already high in emotional intelligence.[7]

Any group that wants to develop team emotional intelligence skills can do so. The hardest part is knowing what to work on. Team emotional intelligence means that members of the team have and use emotional intelligence skills for the good of the group. It does not mean that all team members are emotionally intelligent all of the time. Members of the group are allowed to be human and to have days when they feel discouraged or even overly confident. It's important that other team members balance emotions that may not be realistic or helpful to the situation by helping the group remain aware.

Team members must take time to get to know one another before they can understand one another. One popular technique is to conduct an off-site meeting to discover more about one another's values, interests, talents, and styles. A team can go to lunch or have coffee together as a group. Team members should also check in with one another at the beginning of a meeting and at key points in a design process or any other task they work on together.

Uncomfortable interactions happen for a reason. Teams need to take the time to discover the reason. If one team member is uncomfortable, resisting, or reacting, his or her discomfort should be acknowledged and the person should be told that the entire team is seeking to understand. When the group is uncomfortable with something, someone should recognize the mood in the room and ask, "Why is this so hard for us to discuss?" Usually, the group members will be relieved that they do not have to play along with something they do not agree with or hide their true opinions. A more constructive—or at least genuine—discussion can then follow.

A team can enhance its emotional perspective by focusing more on the bigger picture. If team members have opposing views, the group should discuss these views from each team member's perspective. If everyone agrees, ask, "What are we overlooking? What angle haven't we heard or thought through?" The group or any team member can ask quiet members what they think, and get members who talk a lot to ask questions of others.

When things are uncertain, someone in the group should reinforce the team's confidence in its ability to succeed. This person does not have to be the team leader or even the same person every time. It may be the newest player on the team, the quiet one, or anyone who is willing to engage the team in developing a more positive outlook. Together, team members should focus on what the group can control. They should remind one another of the larger goal and its greater importance than the current disappointment or frustration. They can revisit how the team responded to a previous, similarly difficult situation with good results. They can discuss how to move beyond the emotional pitfalls that hinder teams. Group members can take matters into their own hands to improve their team's emotional intelligence and achieve its greatest goals.

Chapter 8

TAKING EMOTIONAL INTELLIGENCE HOME

EMOTIONALLY INTELLIGENT RELATIONSHIPS

DEEPENING THE CONNECTION WITH YOUR PARTNER

◆

The determining factor in whether wives feel satisfied with sex, romance, and passion in their marriage is, by 70 percent, the quality of the couple's friendship. For men, the determining factor is, by 70 percent, the quality of the couple's friendship. So men and women come from the same planet after all.

JOHN GOTTMAN, PH.D.

My grandfather has been blind most of my life. After several decades of farming the sandy soil in eastern South Dakota, he contracted a disease that destroyed his vision. At ninety-six years of age, he is a captive audience for questions about relationships. He's also a worthy target for my barrage of questions—he's been married to the same person for seventy years. He and my grandmother compare their relationship to their many years spent farming: proper focus plus hard work pulled them through difficult times. More than just sticking with it, they've actively worked together and have reaped the benefits of seven decades of love and companionship.

When they reminisce about the bond that has held them together, they speak of an allegiance to compromise. Whether raising young children during the height of the Great Depression or being trapped indoors for days during the blizzard of '62, they invested energy in repairing arguments as opposed to intensifying them. Even during conflict, they share a commitment to find and understand the other person's perspective. They've always been able to tend to each other as they did their fields of corn—they avoid the slash-and-burn technique at all costs. As an emotionally intelligent couple, they've stayed together as a result of their enduring search for common ground.

Repairs

A new romantic relationship is a lot like buying a car. Driving it off the lot is pure bliss. As you look around, you can scarcely take it all in. Everything smells, sounds, and looks terrific. You coast through weeks—maybe even months—of happy driving before "it" happens for the first time: something breaks, and you need to repair it. Vehicles, like relationships, require repairs to keep them running smoothly. If a car is worth keeping, parts will need to be replaced sometimes. A certain amount of your time and energy will be spent keeping it in tip-top shape. Sometimes there are surprises, but nothing a trip to the mechanic can't fix. Repairs do more than keep your car running; they are the key to an emotionally intelligent relationship. If you don't address the regular wear and tear that accompanies togetherness, you and your partner are sure to find yourselves stuck at the side of the road.

In studies conducted at the University of Washington, Dr. John Gottman and his team of researchers have predicted future divorce with 93 percent accuracy by watching couples for only five minutes to see how often they repair their disagreements.[1] Their predictions have held true for couples they've continued to track a full fourteen years later. This research shows that how often a couple disagrees is irrelevant; it's the effort both partners make to resolve conflict amicably and repair the situation that influences the success of the relationship. Repairs are critical because many disagreements between partners are based on permanent differences of opinion. If you think it's best to shut the air conditioner off at 6 P.M. on hot summer days to save money and your spouse thinks the best time is 8 P.M., neither one of you will ever be right. But that won't stop you from arguing about it all summer long. Disagreements are a given. It's what you do about them that matters.

An emotionally intelligent relationship is driven by two people who focus their energy on repairing their disagreements. Repair means showing love and respect for each other despite the dilemma. When you argue with your partner, every word and every act serves to either make things better or make them worse. Repairs take many forms, but all are aimed at moving the argument to resolution. A repair can be anything from suggesting a compromise ("This summer let's turn the air conditioner off at 7 P.M.") to owning your half of the situation ("I realize that turning it off at 8 P.M. is more expensive") to using humor to break the tension ("You know, this wouldn't be a problem if we lived in Alaska"). A repair attempt sends the powerful signal that you care, you respect your partner, and your love is more important than proving you are right.

Repairs are the biggest sign that emotional intelligence skills are being used in a relationship. But how do you initiate a repair? First, you have to realize that a repair will not solve the disagreement. It is an act of moving beyond the expression of anger, resentment, and hostility toward your partner. The first hope for a successful repair comes from your own self-awareness. You cannot improve an argument if you are being thrown over a barrel by your emotions. Disagreements bring all of your feelings about your partner rushing to the surface, and therefore it can be a real challenge to maintain any sort of perspective on your behavior and emotions. Do not waste time feeling guilty about your feelings in an argument. Focus your energy on understanding your emotions. If you find that your emotions are so strong that you can't think clearly, it is probably best to save the discussion for later. If you are so emotional that you are getting tunnel vision, feeling sick, or just in a haze, the most successful repair may seem like none at all. Explain to your partner that you are overwhelmed and need some time to cool off and get your thoughts together. Your argument is not going anywhere, so you don't need to pressure yourself into a discussion when you can't think clearly.

If you are composed enough to have some perspective on the situation, you can initiate the next step in a repair. Use your social awareness skills to focus your thoughts on what things must be like from your partner's point of view—not what you think they are like but rather what your partner is thinking and feeling. You can't launch a successful repair until you fully understand why your partner is doing whatever it is that he or she is doing. You have to show your partner that you care about how things look from his or her point of view, even if you do not agree with his or her perspective. You need to move beyond thinking of ways to convince your partner of your opinions and ask yourself what you can do to honor his or her feelings. Showing respect for your partner's opinions whether they are right or wrong—is the key to compromise.

The appearance of a successful repair is as varied as the problems it can solve. A repair that works in one situation, with one person, may just make things worse in another. Saying "What exactly do you mean by that?" can sound as though you are minimizing the issues during one argument but be received as a sign of wanting to make things better during another. To repair successfully, arm yourself with the knowledge that many attempts will crash and burn. Even an empathetic comment such as, "I understand what you are saying" can be perceived as belittling if your partner is defensive or not accustomed to your saying this. Be ready to try a number of repairs in a single argument and expect that they will not all go off without a hitch. A failed repair attempt can create hurt feelings and bruised egos. Lean into your discomfort and work to tolerate the pain that surfaces when your partner misunderstands your efforts to make things better. The more you do so, the more he or she will be receptive and do the same. Couples with the best skill at repairing disagreements are those who try to do so the most often. Your repeated attempts at empathy and understanding will not be lost on a loving, committed partner.

It will also help your relationship to discuss repairs together. If you can talk about your arguments, you are both more likely to initiate repairs the next time you fight. When repair attempts are always one-sided, the relationship usually fails. Both partners need to work toward resolving their disagreements. When you talk to your partner about repairs, you develop an understanding that you will both use them during your next argument. Even if your partner has trouble making repairs the next time the two of you argue, he or she will likely recognize your effort and realize that it is an attempt to show concern and make things better.

Use your emotional intelligence skills to discuss and repair arguments. You must know yourself and understand your feelings throughout the argument. This means being self-aware enough to recognize when you can tolerate initiating a repair. You need to use your social awareness skills to "read" the other person, and the argument will go more smoothly if you self-manage throughout. Repairs don't require both partners to act with emotional intelligence. Sometimes just one partner will have the perspective to self-manage and initiate a repair. When the other responds in kind, the relationship builds an unshakable strength that can only come from emotional intelligence.

Emotionally Intelligent Parenting

RAISING A HAPPY CHILD

◆

The joys of parents are secret, and so are their griefs and fears.

FRANCIS BACON

Jim Carrey had a difficult childhood. His family was quite poor, and while other sixteen-year-olds were going to high school and playing sports, Jim worked with his family in a wheel factory and even spent a year living out of their van. Humor was Jim's salvation. He could bend his face into silly positions that left everyone laughing hysterically. His father, Percy, was supportive of his son's unique ability to "escape" from the challenges of daily living.[2] More than anything, Percy wanted Jim to feel comfortable living in his own flexible skin.

At fourteen, Jim's comedic talents led to a night trying stand-up comedy at Yuk Yuk's, a local comedy club. Jim wanted desperately to perform, but he was terrified the week before the event over how his jokes would be received by strangers. Recognizing Jim's fear, his dad spent hours helping him practice his act. Percy wanted Jim to work through his anxiety and build it into confidence, and he knew a fourteen-year-old could not do this on his own. They went to the club together that night, but Jim bombed onstage alone. Despite that setback, Percy convinced Jim to continue pursuing comedy.[3]

By age nineteen, Jim was back onstage and even became a regular on the Canadian comedy circuit. Laughing audiences confirmed what his father told him all along—Jim was funny—but he knew the real test for any comedian was in Hollywood, so he packed his belongings and headed for California. It didn't take long for Jim to realize he was suddenly a little fish in a very big pond. After two years of playing bad gigs and living in seedy motels, Jim gave up and went back to

Canada. Back at home, Percy reminded Jim that he was a phenomenal talent, yet he had to persist at any level if he wanted to succeed.[4]

When Jim returned to Los Angeles, he often drove his clunky car up Mulholland Drive and parked on a hill overlooking Hollywood. One evening, fueled by his father's belief in his comedic talent, he wrote himself a check for $10 million. The memo read, "For acting services rendered."

By the time Percy died, years later, Jim was the first actor ever to receive $20 million for starring in a film. Jim's grief was intense at his father's funeral. When it was Jim's turn to approach the casket, he decided to express his gratitude for his father's love. Jim leaned over Percy, whispered a final good-bye, and slipped the check for $10 million into his suit pocket, the symbol of the ardent support he had carried all these years.

A parent has the single greatest opportunity to influence his child's emotional intelligence. Percy Carrey's patient guidance did far more for Jim than helping him to understand his talents. His support reinforced Jim's ability to lean into the discomfort that comes with rejection and to believe in himself. Percy taught his son self-management, knowing it was the skill he would need most to realize his tremendous potential. Emotional intelligence skills are made, not born. A parent's guidance in understanding and processing emotions is the driving force behind a child's ultimate ability to demonstrate emotional intelligence.

We have heard it said that an empathetic manager can't help but be empathic at home with her children as well. As obvious as this may sound, it simply isn't true. There are no guarantees of consistency between how we behave in our personal life and our professional life. People do a great job of drawing a line between these roles. A charismatic, motivating manager may be very disconnected in her relationship with a son or daughter. The empathy and understanding she uses to connect with her staff and win over customers can quickly disappear when she's back home trying to get a squirming three-year-old into his pajamas. A sincere motivationto develop emotional intelligence skills can—and should—cross the artificial boundary that so many of us erect between how we are at work and how we are at home.

The challenges you face as a parent don't have to determine your child's emotional intelligence. A study conducted at Emory University showed how a child's emotional intelligence is a product of the parents' demonstration of emotional intelligence skills, not their personal experience of emotional distress.[5] Children learn emotional intelligence skills from their parents. Without the example of their parents, children miss out on the best source to learn from. Every moment you spend with your child is an opportunity to demonstrate emotional intelligence. When you refrain from yelling, your child will also. When you notice and ask about your child's sad feelings, your child will learn to show sympathy for friends.

Parents who practice emotional intelligence with their children raise boys and girls who are happier and better socially adjusted, get better grades, and later achieve a higher level of professional success.[6] Children who increase their emotional intelligence skills decrease their levels of truancy and delinquent behavior. Regardless of where a child starts, increasing her emotional intelligence improves her connection with her peers and reduces her experimentation with alcohol and tobacco.[7] If you model emotional intelligence for your children, they will develop the skills they need to get along better with others, and they will experience a greater level of success that will last into adulthood.

Coaching Through Conflict

Most kids display mood swings that appear wider, deeper, and quicker than those of adults. Ask any parents of a two-and-a-half-year-old, and they will describe giddy bliss one minute morphing into utter despair the next. During that magical four-to-seven-year range, parents enjoy their children's increasing use of words to say what they feel, but they also become involved in extended dramas about seemingly trivial matters. Preadolescents begin to take charge of what they do with how they feel. Adolescents feel sophisticated emotions (and hormones!) for which their life experiences haven't yet prepared them. Each phase of raising children is characterized by strong emotions that surface in new ways. At every age, emotions catch developing children and parents by surprise. To develop emotional intelligence skills, your child must feel permitted—even invited—to experience these emotions fully and learn to understand them.

To help children understand their emotions, you first have to make it okay for them to have them. Embracing your child's emotions is often a simple and unremarkable act. If you make it your duty, the cumulative impact on your child will be profound. Embracing your daughter's feelings can be as simple as saying "It hurts to lose your favorite blanket" instead of "Stop crying. We can get another one." The first statement tells her that her feelings are normal and important. Neither statement takes away the pain of losing the blanket; her crying will continue either way. But the first response models emotional awareness and teaches that what she thinks and feels is valid. Young children can't contemplate events in any sophisticated way, but their minds soak up their experiences like a sponge. You shape your child each day by teaching her how to deal with her feelings.

Embracing your child's emotions is hardest to do when it's needed most. Emotions erupt during conflicts that put parents on edge. When your child does something that is foolish and beneath his capability, it can be hard to avoid pouncing on the situation like a panther. When your three-year-old cracks the neighbor boy on the head with a toy for refusing to share, you probably won't be inclined to lean over and murmur, "I understand that you feel angry, honey, but it's not acceptable to smack Johnny on the head with your truck." We realize that such a response isn't realistic in most situations, so you will have to send the message to your child in other ways. Your tone, your speed in acting, and even what you do teaches your child about emotions. A response that shows you understand your child's anger (everybody gets angry, right?) will teach him more about controlling himself the next time than grabbing him by the arm and dragging him out of the room.

Conflict and passive resistance generate strong emotions in parents, too. It can be just as annoying to watch your child make herself vulnerable as it can to watch her hurt another kid. But careful consideration of the situation shows that children express their feelings through their actions. This is normal—toddlers hit other children or stand paralyzed by others' aggression until they learn a better way to express themselves. Your job is to model comfort with emotions and coach your child through doing something productive with them. As the parent, using your emotional intelligence skills increases the likelihood that your children will do the same when faced with challenges. The results of your efforts, however difficult the act may feel at the time, are long-term. Your children will grow into adults who know how to enhance their relationships and manage their behavior to get what they want out of life.

Coaching a child through her emotions is every bit as challenging and uncomfortable as facing your own. Like so many things in life, if we don't act carefully we are bound to repeat old patterns. Progress comes from choosing the response that is the most effective over that which is easiest and most readily available. Emotional intelligence offers a profound opportunity to build a new perspective on everything that's important in your life. Increasing your emotional intelligence is simply a matter of waking up to the emotions that drive you. When you know them well, you can make your own decisions about where they will take you.

Living with Emotional Intelligence

You're probably wondering what you should do with everything you've learned from this book. We've presented ideas rapidly with the sincere hope that you'll spend your time developing new skills, rather than reading about them. Emotional intelligence is a product of how well you understand yourself and those around you. You can't learn that by studying models, memorizing facts, or reading motivational prose. Your emotional intelligence profile will be your guide to which skills are your strengths as well as what you need to work on most. Study your results from the Emotional Intelligence Appraisal carefully—they are a window to your current level of emotional intelligence.

It shouldn't take much time from your day to work on the emotional intelligence skills you've learned. You can practice them anytime. Thinking differently for just a split second in response to a challenge can take you down a fresh path. If you practice a new skill repeatedly, you'll train your brain into making it a habit. Practice one skill in every area of your life—at home, at work, at school, with friends, in your community. Improved emotional intelligence should carry over into everything you do. You will no longer have to try to make your feelings go away. You will have all the knowledge you need to exercise patience, perseverance, and perspective in every aspect of your life. You have the power of emotional intelligence on your side . . . and you always will.

Appendix

A TECHNICAL REPORT ON THE EMOTIONAL INTELLIGENCE APPRAISAL

◆

Jean H. Riley, M.S.,
Quinn D. Sanders, M.S.,
Lac D. Su, M.S.,
and April D. West, M.S.

TalentSmart Psychometric
Research Team

Anytime you use a psychological test, it is critical to understand how it was developed, as well as some of the finer points of how the test works. For a test to be valid for the purpose at hand, research is conducted to confirm the quality of the questions, including how scores connect to important outcomes. The Emotional Intelligence Appraisal is set to the highest standards set forth by the American Psychological Association.[1]

What is the Emotional Intelligence Appraisal?

It is a survey suite that measures emotional intelligence (EQ) quickly and accurately. The original aim of the test was to provide a quick, valid, and intuitive assessment of EQ that would be readily available to the public and based on the prevailing model. We refer to this as a survey suite because it comes in three editions: the Me Edition (a self-assessment), the Multi-Rater (MR) Edition (360-degree feedback from coworkers, friends, or family), and the Team Edition (the collective EQ of an intact work group). An online administration of the self-assessment (the Me Edition) can be accessed by using the unique code provided on the inside cover of this book. The Emotional Intelligence Appraisal provides scores and easy-to-understand recommendations that are customized to fit the user's unique skill profile. The test measures overall emotional intelligence and scores in the four key skill areas with just twenty-eight questions.

The average administration time for the online edition of the test is seven minutes. The online format contains a complete test and interactive e-learning using Hollywood movies, goal tracking, and dynamic action plans. Each copy of *The Emotional Intelligence Quick Book* includes a unique code on the reverse side of the book jacket that you will need in order to take the test online.

What theory of emotional intelligence is the Emotional Intelligence Appraisal based on?

It measures emotional intelligence using Daniel Goleman's model, as introduced in *Primal Leadership*.[2] This theory is grounded in the idea that emotional intelligence is subdivided into four skills: self-awareness, self-management, social awareness, and relationship management, with these skills rolling up into personal and social competence. The test provides an overall EQ score, a score for personal and social competence, and a score for each of the four skills. Strong intercorrelations among the four skills reveal personal and social competence as the most accurate emotional intelligence scores, other than the overall EQ score.[3] The four skills lack the construct validity needed to stand as independent components, but they are intuitive to retain and follow, so they are also provided as face-valid components of EQ.

Is the information I enter secure?

Yes. All responses to the test are stored on a secure remote server. TalentSmart monitors our servers twenty-four hours a day to ensure that no one will have access to your results or saved comments.

Does my test expire?

Your results do not expire. Once you take the test, you will have immediate access to your results and can come back and see them online anytime you wish.

Does the Emotional Intelligence Appraisal focus only on work situations?

The questions are worded to apply broadly to a variety of situations. You can use the Emotional Intelligence Appraisal to evaluate your emotional intelligence at work or at home. Most people tend to behave differently at work than they do at home and vice versa. In most instances it is best to pick one setting (work or home) before beginning the test and keep that frame of mind while answering the questions.

Why is the scale 0 to 100?

The 100-point scale is used because of the familiarity this range holds for people. The majority of people has attended education systems where the same range of scores was applied to their evaluations. It's much easier for someone to compare a score of 77 in one skill to a 93 in another than it is to compare the equivalent raw scores (a 4.2 and a 5.1). While there is no absolute level of mastery for emotional intelligence skills (these skills can always be developed further), it is accepted that the higher you score, the better you are at using emotional intelligence skills.

What is the average range of scores?

Scores on the Emotional Intelligence Appraisal are normally distributed, with a mean score of 75. This means that the majority (68 percent) of scores will fall in the middle of the range (between 65 and 85) and fewer scores will fall at the extreme high or low ends of the scale. This is important because this type of scale is different from scores in school, where "average" is often perceived negatively. Scoring within the average range on this test is to be anticipated.

How can the Emotional Intelligence Appraisal be accurate with only twenty-eight questions?

Skill tests tend to be long and cumbersome. They often exceed 100 questions, and this makes taking them a chore. Contrary to common belief, skill tests do not require large numbers of questions to accurately measure a single skill. The tradition of lengthy tests has more to do with the subject feeling as if he or she has been accurately assessed than the accuracy or usefulness of the test.[4] The Emotional Intelligence Appraisal measures primarily one skill, emotional intelligence. Therefore, a test of emotional intelligence doesn't require a large number of questions. A parallel example is the Beck Depression Inventory (BDI), the most trusted measure of depression available. The BDI measures depression (a single construct) with just thirteen questions. The Emotional Intelligence Appraisal accomplishes a similar feat by measuring the two constructs of emotional intelligence (personal and social competence) with just twenty-eight questions,[5] and it doesn't require prerequisite education or training to use.

Is the Emotional Intelligence Appraisal reliable and valid?

The Emotional Intelligence Appraisal is both reliable and valid. Reliability refers to whether the test is consistent over time, while validity refers to whether the test is measuring what it is intended to measure. The internal consistency reliability figures for the skills measured by the test range from .85 to .91, a strong indication that the test is reliable. The standard level of acceptable reliability is .70 or greater. Analyses of construct validity suggest that the best fit for the model is an overall EQ score with division along the lines of personal and social competence. A series of specialized analyses (principal component analysis, Catell's scree test, Kaiser-Meyer-Oklin, and Bartlett's test of sphericity) each indicate that personal and social competence are the main factors in emotional intelligence.[6]

In studies measuring emotional intelligence and job performance, the Emotional Intelligence Appraisal explains a highly significant amount of the variance in job performance for people holding a variety of positions.[7] Across studies, the Me Edition (self-report) explains a significant amount (nearly 20 percent) of the variance in job performance, and the Multi-Rater Edition (360-degree report) explains a highly significant amount (nearly 60 percent) of performance. An analysis comparing leaders' emotional intelligence scores on the test to key financial indicators shows that leaders who are high in emotional intelligence are 20 percent more productive than their low-EQ counterparts. This amounts to $250,000 more productivity for those leaders high in EQ.

How were the questions designed?

Dr. Bradberry and Dr. Greaves, with years of subject matter expertise and applied assessment development experience, developed a pool of questions for each of the four skill scales. The authors used an iterative process of writing draft questions and reworking them to ensure that they passed the test of being both "necessary and sufficient." The term "necessary" refers to all questions that are required to measure a skill, and the term "sufficient" refers to only those questions that are required to measure the skill. In other words, no extra questions were added to the test and no questions that were required were missing from the test. Once the set of questions met the face-validity criteria, they were presented to other subject matter experts. Questions were removed that didn't contribute to the face validity of the test as determined by the subject matter experts. Next, questions were removed that didn't contribute to the statistical validity of the test.

The final length of the test is based solely on what is necessary and sufficient to measure your emotional intelligence. Dr. Bradberry's and Dr. Greaves's approach to writing questions improves upon two important drawbacks to the pure behavioral description approach. First, the test questions do not attempt to measure *every* example of the behaviors that make up a skill. The questions avoid this redundancy by describing critical aspects of each skill that indicate its presence.

Skill statements on the Emotional Intelligence Appraisal are rated on a frequency scale, ranging from "Never" to "Always." People tend to have a good idea of how often they demonstrate different behaviors. The key benefit of this approach is that it measures the same skill as other tests of emotional intelligence but with fewer questions.

How was the Emotional Intelligence Appraisal normed?

Normative samples are descriptive standards against which individuals can compare their performance to the performance of other people.[8] The test uses external norms, meaning that an individual's score is compared to the scores of more than 100,000 other people. The normative sample includes male and female subjects ages eighteen to eighty-plus years, working in every industry and every job function worldwide. All subjects completed the English-language edition of the test.

Does the Emotional Intelligence Appraisal reduce self-serving bias?

Self-serving bias is the tendency to enhance self-scoring

by taking credit for success and denying responsibility for failure. All self-report tests are subject to such bias, and the goal is to minimize this as much as possible. The Emotional Intelligence Appraisal employs rigorous methods that greatly reduce this bias. The only surefire way to eliminate the bias is to collect the observations of other people. To this end, the Multi-Rater Edition of the test is available.

Why is the e-learning included?

Tests are supposed to be learning tools. Simply determining your score is not enough if you wish to develop a new, dynamic skill such as emotional intelligence. E-learning lets you see the skill in action, which increases the motivation to learn.

Should the Emotional Intelligence Appraisal be used for employee selection?

TalentSmart, Inc. does not promote, recommend, or support the use of the test for selection and hiring purposes. Though the test is a valid and reliable measure of emotional intelligence, it's not intended to select candidates for a job. The test is a training and development tool that should be used to increase the emotional intelligence skills of your current staff.

Notes

1 The Discovery

1. Dr. John Harlow, "Passage of an Iron Rod Through the Head," *Boston Medical and Surgical Journal* 39 (1848): 506–507. Dr. John Harlow, "Recovery from the Passage of an Iron Bar Through the Head," *Publications of the Massachusetts Medical Society* 2 (1868).
2. Harlow, "Recovery."
3. Proverbs, 6, 14–16; Epistle of Paul to the Colossians, 3, and First Epistle of Peter, 1; Aristotle, *The Nicomachean Ethics;* John Cooper et al., *The Complete Works of Plato* (Indianapolis, Ind.: Hacket, 1997); William Shakespeare, *The Oxford Shakespeare: The Complete Works* (New York: Oxford University Press, 1966). Re Thomas Jefferson: http://etext.virginia.edu/jefferson/quotations/jeff0200.htm.
4. E. L. Thorndike, "Intelligence and Its Uses," *Harper's Magazine* 140 (1920): 227–335.
5. W. L. Payne, "A Study of Emotion: Developing Emotional Intelligence: Self Integration; Relating to Fear, Pain and Desire," doctoral dissertation, Union Institute, Cincinnati, Ohio (1988).
6. Jack Mayer et al., "Perceiving Affective Content in Ambiguous Visual Stimuli: A Component of Emotional Intelligence," *Journal of Personality Assessment* 54 (1990): 772–81.
   Jack Mayer and Peter Salovey, "The Intelligence of Emotional Intelligence," *Intelligence* 17 (1993): 433–42.
   Jack Mayer and A. Stevens, "An Emerging Understanding of the Reflective (Meta) Experience of Mood," *Journal of Research in Personality* 28 (1994): 351–73.
7. The emotional intelligence model of Goleman, Boyatzis, and McKee in *Primal Leadership: Realizing the Power of Emotional Intelligence* (Boston: Harvard Business School Press, 2002), groups the four skills (self-awareness, self-management, social awareness, and relationship management) into the larger categories of personal and social competence. Our research confirms personal and social competence as being the most accurate division of emotional intelligence into parts.

Notes

2 Amazing EQ

1. Lisa Yoon, "On Boards, Are Women the Fairer Sex?" *Chief Financial Officer* magazine, online edition, www.cfo.com/printable/article.cfm/3009002?f=options. Israel Helfand, "What Lies Behind the Anger in Men," *The Northwest Recovery Networker,* March 1992.
2. Mike Lancaster, "Fox Pulls Plug on Ailing 'Magic Hour': Johnson Sent to Showers After Meager Eight-Week Run," www.thestinkers.com/Philadelphia Newspapers, Inc., August 7, 1998.
3. Quotes from Craig Shoemaker describing his experience on *The Magic Hour* from a radio interview on *The Paul Harris Show* are available at www.harrisonline.com.
4. Lancaster, "Fox Pulls Plug on Ailing 'Magic Hour.'"
5. Dr. Joseph Ciarrochi, et al., "Emotional Intelligence Moderates the Relationship Between Stress and Mental Health," *Personality and Individual Differences* 32 (2002): 197–209. Dennis R. Trinidad, "The Association Between Emotional Intelligence and Early Adolescent Tobacco and Alcohol Use," *Personality and Individual Differences* 32 (2002): 95–105.
6. Marc A. Brackett et al., "Emotional Intelligence and Its Relation to Everyday Behavior," *Personality and Individual Differences* 36 (2004): 1387–1402. Benjamin Palmer et al., "Emotional Intelligence and Life Satisfaction," *Personality and Individual Differences* 33 (2002): 1091–1100. Adrian Furnham, "Trait Emotional Intelligence and Happiness," *Social Behavior & Personality* 31 (2003): 815–24.
7. Shankar Vedantam, "Stress Found to Weaken Resistance to Illness," *The Washington Post,* December 22, 2003.
8. Ibid.
9. Joel B. Finkelstein, "Ability to Cope with Stress May Play a Role in Cancer Progression," *Health Behavior News Service,* December 1, 2002. "Animal Research Suggests That Stress May Increase Risk of Uterine Cancer," Wake Forest University Medical Center Press Release, July 9, 2004.
10. "Study Ties Stress to Breast Cancer," *Discovery Health News,* September 24, 2003, available at www.hon.ch/News/HSN/515236.html.
11. American Heart Association, "New Stats Show Heart Disease Still America's No. 1 Killer, Stroke No. 3," *Heart Disease and Stroke Statistics—2004 Update,* January 2004.

12. Bishop et al., "AHA Scientific Sessions, Chicago," *Archives of General Psychiatry* 50 (November 2002): 681–89. B. Anderson et al., "Psychological, Behavioral, and Immune Changes After a Psychological Intervention: A Clinical Trial," *Journal of Clinical Oncology* 22 (2004): 3570–80.
13. Ibid.
14. Bishop, "AHA Scientific Sessions."
15. B. A. van der Kolk, "The Body Keeps the Score: Memory and the Emerging Psychobiology of Post Traumatic Stress," *Harvard Review of Psychiatry* 1 (1994): 253–65. B. A. van der Kolk et al., "Dissociation, Somatization, and Affect Dysregulation: The Complexity of Adaptation of Trauma," *American Journal of Psychiatry* 153 (1996): 83–93.
16. Neil M. Ashkanasy, "The Case for Emotional Intelligence in Workgroups," symposium presentation at the annual conference of the Society for Industrial and Organizational Psychology, San Diego, Calif., April 11, 2001.Peter Jordan et al., "The Case for Emotional Intelligence in Organizational Research," *Academy of Management Review* 28 (2003): 195–97.
17. The U.S. Air Force saved $3 million in training costs by selecting civilian recruiters for their emotional intelligence: "Military Recruiting: The Department of Defense Could Improve Its Recruiter Selection and Incentive Systems," General Accounting Office Report 98-58, January 30, 1998, www.gao.gov/archive/1998/ns98058.pdf. L'Oréal salespeople selected for their emotional intelligence skills were responsible for $91,370 more sales per head with 63 percent less turnover; Spencer and Spencer, *Competence at Work: Models for Superior Performance* (New York: John Wiley and Sons, 1993).

4 Important Questions

1. Francis Hesselbein et al., *The Leader of the Future* (San Francisco: Jossey-Bass, 1997).

5 Changing Your Mind

1. T. P. Pons et al., "Massive Cortical Reorganization After Sensory Deafferentation in Adult Macaques," *Science* 252 (June 28, 1991): 1858–59. N. Jain, "Deactivation and Reactivation of Somatosensory Cortex Is Accompanied by Reductions in GABA Straining,

Somatosensory & Motor Research 8 (1997): 347–54. D. Borsook et al., "Acute Plasticity in the Human Somatosensory Cortex Following Amputation," *NeuroReport* 9 (1998): 1013–17.

2. General Nutrition Centers, reported by the Associated Press: http://pittsburgh.about.com/cs/holidays/tp/ resolutions.htm.
3. Richard Boyatzis et al., "Will It Make a Difference?: Assessing a Value-Added, Outcome-Oriented, Competency-Based Professional Program," in *Innovation in Professional Education: Steps on a Journey from Teaching to Learning* (San Francisco: Jossey-Bass, 1995), 167–202.

6 Building Your Skills

1. Ray Charles's reflections on his life and accomplishments are found on his Web site: www.raycharles.com/autobio.htm.
2. www.raycharles.com/autobio.
3. Ibid.
4. Peter Drucker, "Managing Oneself," *The Harvard Business Review* (March 1999): 66–67.
5. Table of emotions reproduced and adapted with permission from Julia West at www.sff.net/people/julia.west/CALLIHOO/ dtbb/feelings.htm.
6. O. Ayduk and W. Mischel, "When Smart People Behave Stupidly: Reconciling Inconsistencies in Social-Emotional Intelligence," in *Why Smart People Can Be So Stupid,* edited by Robert J. Sternberg (New Haven, Conn.: Yale University Press, 2002).
7. R. D. Grainger, "The Use—and Abuse—of Negative Thinking," *American Journal of Nursing* 91 (1991): 13–14.

7 Bringing Emotional Intelligence to Work

1. Joseph L. Badaracco, Jr., *Defining Moments: When Managers Must Choose Between Right and Right* (Boston: Harvard Business School Press, 1997).
2. A detailed account of decision making is listed in NASA's Columbia Accident Investigation Board Report, vol. 1, August 2003, Chapter 8, "History as Cause: *Columbia* and *Challenger,*" 195–204.
3. Roger Boisjoly, "Roger Boisjoly and the *Challenger* Disaster." Online Ethics Center for Engineering and Science, Case Western Reserve University: www.onlineethics.org/moral/boisjoly/RB1-6.html.

4. Vanessa Urch Druskat and Steven B. Wolff. "Building the Emotional Intelligence of Groups," *The Harvard Business Review* (March 2001): 79–90.
5. Neil M. Ashkanasy, "The Case for Emotional Intelligence in Workgroups," symposium presentation at the annual conference of the Society for Industrial and Organizational Psychology, San Diego, Calif., April 11, 2001.
6. "*Pressures on the System," Report of the Presidential Commission on the Space Shuttle* Challenger *Accident,* vol. 1 (Washington, D.C.: U.S. Government Printing Office, 1986): 171–73.
7. Ashkanasy, "The Case for Emotional Intelligence in Workgroups."

8 Taking Emotional Intelligence Home

1. John Gottman and Robert W. Levenson, "Rebound from Marital Conflict and Divorce Prediction," *Family Process* 38 (1999): 287–92. John Gottman and Robert W. Levenson, "A Two-Factor Model for Predicting When a Couple Will Divorce: Exploratory Analyses Using 14-Year Longitudinal Data," *Family Process* 41 (2002): 83–96.
2. Nancy Krulik, *Fun and Funnier: Jim Carrey* (New York: Simon & Schuster, 2000).
3. Jim Carrey's first attempts at comedy and quotes from his night at Yuk Yuk's are from an interview on *E* online: www.eonline.com/On/Revealed/Shows/Carrey/index2.html.
4. Jim Carrey story of surviving in Hollywood and quote on failure are from Andrew O'Hehir, "The Jim Carrey Show," on Salon.com, December 7, 1999.
5. Michelle Broth, "Associations Between Mothers' Negative Emotionality and Stress and Their Socialization of Emotion Practices: Mothers' *Emotional* Competence as Resiliency or Risk," *Dissertation Abstracts International* 64 (2004): 4025.
6. John Gottman, *Raising an Emotionally Intelligent Child* (New York: Fireside Books, 1997).
7. "Why Teach Social and Emotional Skills?" the Committee for Children Web site, www.cfchildren.org. Impact of emotional intelligence programs on children: PBS NewsHour on Emotional Intelligence, November 27, 1997. Link between emotional intelligence in children and alcohol and drug use: Dennis R. Trinidad, "The Association Between Emotional Intelligence and

Early Adolescent Tobacco and Alcohol Use," *Personality and Individual Differences* 32 (January 2002): 95–105.

Appendix: A Technical Report on the Emotional Intelligence Appraisal

1. The standards for assessment development and validation as set forth by the American Psychological Association can be found in *Standards for Educational and Psychological Testing* (Washington, D.C.: American Psychological Association, 1999).
2. D. Goleman, R. Boyatsis, and A. McKee, *Primal Leadership* (Boston: Harvard Business School Publishing, 2002).
3. T. Bradberry and J. Greaves, *The Emotional Intelligence Appraisal™ Technical Manual* (San Diego: TalentSmart, Inc., 2002); available at www.TalentSmart.com/learn.
4. P. B. Sheatsley, "Questionnaire Construction and Item Writing," in *Handbook of Survey Research,* edited by P. H. Rossi, J. D. Wright, and A. B. Anderson (San Diego, Calif.: Academic Press, 1983), pp. 195–230.
5. A. T. Beck, W. Y. Rial, and K. Rickets, "Short Form of Depression Inventory: Cross-Validation," *Psychological-Reports* 34 (1974): 1184–86; A. T. Beck, R. A. Steer, and M. G. Garbin, "Psychometric Properties of the Beck Depression Inventory: Twenty-five Years of Evaluation," *Clinical Psychology Review* 8 (1988): 77–100.
6. R. B. Catell, "The Scree Test for Number of Factors," *Multivariate Behavioral Research* 1 (1966): 245–76. H. Kaiser, "A Second Generation Little Jiffy," *Psychometrika* 35 (1970): 401–15. M.S. Bartlett, "A Note on Multiplying Factors for Various Chi-Square Approximations," *Journal of the Royal Statistical Society* 16 (Series B) (1954): 296–98.
7. Bradberry and Greaves, *The Emotional Intelligence Appraisal Technical Manual.*
8. G. W. Morris, and M. A. Lo Verde, "Consortium Surveys," in *Improving Organizational Surveys: New Directions, Methods, and Applications,* edited by P. Rosenfeld, J. E. Edwards, and M. D. Thomas (Newbury Park, Calif.: Sage, 1993), 122–42.

Discussion Questions

Discussing emotional intelligence will help you bridge the learning–doing gap. Use these questions to start a meaningful dialogue and build your understanding of how the four emotional intelligence skills apply in daily living. For additional discussion questions and other group learning tools, visit www.EIQuickbook.com.

1. *How many members in the group knew about the term "emotional intelligence" before reading* The Emotional Intelligence Quick Book?
2. *For those who had never heard of emotional intelligence before, what's the most important thing you discovered after reading* The Emotional Intelligence Quick Book?
3. *For those who were familiar with emotional intelligence before reading the book, what's the most important thing you discovered?*
4. *Which story from the book meant the most to you? Why?*
5. *What's one story from your own life that illustrates an interesting element of emotional intelligence? Each member who wishes to can share a story.*
6. *Would you do anything differently if you were in that situation again?*
7. *Which of the four emotional intelligence skills (self-awareness, self-management, social awareness, or*

relationship management) comes easiest for you? Which one takes more effort?

For groups that decide to take the online Emotional Intelligence Appraisal test beforehand, you can bring your results and discuss them as follows.

8. *Without sharing specific numbers, which emotional intelligence score was your highest?*
9. *Was your highest score much higher than the others, or were they relatively equal?*
10. *Thinking back on growing up, what's one experience that stands out for you in learning to recognize or manage your emotions? What about learning to recognize what other people are feeling and going through?*
11. *What is an example from your life where you felt your emotions getting the best of you? What triggered the feelings? What happens to you physically when you feel this way?*
12. *Looking back on it, how do you feel about it now? What happened as a result of your feelings?*
13. *What two lessons will you take away and try to implement after reading* The Emotional Intelligence Quick Book?
14. *What will make practicing emotional intelligence skills most challenging for you?*
15. *What would you like to know from the other people in the group about how they:*

- Work on being more self-aware?
- Self-manage?
- Read feelings or emotions in other people?
- Manage relationships?

16. *In your job, how are emotions dealt with? Is there anything covered in the book that will help you in the next six months at work? How about the next week?*
17. *How are emotional intelligence skills visible in current events today? Discuss politicians, celebrities, athletes, etc.*
18. *Can your group think of any historical figures or events that were influenced by either poor management or excellent management of emotions?*
19. *Think of the teacher who had the greatest influence on your life. How did this person approach emotions?*

Acknowledgments

The body of research supporting this book is the result of a tremendous effort by the bright and dedicated team of behavioral scientists at TalentSmart. We wish to thank the backbone of this group by name and offer our sincerest expression of gratitude for their effort and commitment: Jean Riley, Quinn Sanders, Lac Su, and April West. Their leadership, combined with the efforts of the rest of the research team, have been tremendous.

We would also like to thank everyone at TalentSmart for creating such a tremendous place to come to work each day. Thank you to Shauna Tillman-Mangan for dedicating herself to public relations for this book. She is instrumental to its success and has been a real asset from the moment she took the job. We have worked with a slew of programmers, none of whom could match the skill, perseverance, and leadership of Les Brown.

Tremendous gratitude to our editor, Nancy Hancock, Sarah Peach, Lisa Sciambra, and the entire team at Simon & Schuster for embracing this book. We received invaluable feedback as we wrote the manuscript and wish to thank the following individuals: Paul Brooks, Lilia Corpuz, Mark Greaves, Joyce Haak, Richard La China, Greg Olmstead, Giles Raymond, Antoinette Thomas, and Diane Wolfe. A big thank-you to Dawn Sanders at Urban-Digital.com for creating the wonderful illustrations in this book.

We would like to thank those who have come before us in this field. We are proud to be a part of the emotional intelligence community. We wish to acknowledge the work of Daniel Goleman and are grateful for the use of his highly practical model of emotional intelligence. We must also thank Peter Salovey, a man who is not only an impressive and enviable practitioner but also the epitome of high emotional intelligence.

Thank you to all of the TalentSmart certified trainers and clients who have launched emotional intelligence initiatives in their organizations. Their insights have been a major contribution to this book. We also appreciate the five-hundred-thousand-plus individuals who have participated in our applied research during the last decade.

I, Jean, thank my husband, Greg, for his unwavering love, his honest perspectives, and the extra family responsibilities he carried during key phases of completing this book. Claire and Ingrid are my little loves, and I appreciate how patient and understanding they were while I wrote.

I, Travis, thank my wife for providing support and encouragement in the pursuit of my passion. I thought it was only fitting that I began the chapter on relationships sitting next to you on an airplane. If you remember that day, I was in the window seat, which you had given up so I could have more elbow room to write. I know that you live for the window seat and offered it to me as a gesture of your support for this project. That ride was a great metaphor for your support all along the way, and I am really glad you didn't get sick from the turbulence! Thank you so very much for everything. You are a bedrock of strength that helps me to fulfill my dreams. Here's to a smooth ride with a nice view from here to wherever we go together. I love you.

Index

Index

About TalentSmart

The authors are the cofounders of TalentSmart, the leading provider of emotional intelligence tests, training, and consulting. They offer an array of products and services to organizations worldwide, including a newsletter and free articles and white papers through their Web site. TalentSmart offers the following:

Emotional Intelligence Keynotes

Have one of the authors deliver a dynamic presentation in your organization that will introduce emotional intelligence and inspire change and commitment.

Emotional Intelligence Training

Take part in the most dynamic and engaging emotional intelligence training program available. TalentSmart trainers teach through assessment, interactive exercises, and blockbuster Hollywood movies in a blended solution with bottom-line impact.

Emotional Intelligence Certification

Get certified to deliver the TalentSmart emotional intelligence training program. Certification sessions run regularly across the country. Visit www.talentsmart.com/eqcert.

BRAINS! Emotional Intelligence Training Video

No more boring training videos! Brings emotional intelligence to life for your group using Hollywood movies, television, and historical events.

Emotional Intelligence PowerPoint

A complete 23-slide presentation that introduces emotional intelligence and reviews the latest research and skill development strategies.

Emotional Intelligence Structured Interviewing Guide

Eighty percent of successful hires have one thing in common: a high EQ. Walks hiring managers and HR staff through interviewing and choosing candidates high in emotional intelligence.

To inquire about these and other solutions, contact us at:

www.TalentSmart.com
(888) 818-SMART

About the Authors

Drs. Travis Bradberry and Jean Greaves are the founders of TalentSmart, the leading provider of emotional intelligence tests, products, and training. Their established reputation in the field of psychological testing includes coauthorship with Dr. Ken Blanchard, the top-selling business author of all time and coauthor of *The One Minute Manager.*

Dr. Bradberry is a captivating speaker and consultant, improving the performance of people and organizations around the globe. His work has assisted leaders of Fortune 500 companies, all three branches of government including the U.S. Senate, and even royalty abroad. He holds a dual doctorate in clinical and industrial-organizational psychology.

Dr. Greaves is an award-winning consultant, entrepreneur, and coach with twenty years' experience helping organizations and people fulfill their potential. She specializes in challenging periods of rapid growth, with a third of the Fortune 500 having benefited from her expertise. She holds a doctorate in industrial-organizational psychology.